Collins

need to know?

Downloading

David McCandless

Collins

First published in 2006 by Collins
an imprint of
HarperCollins Publishers
77–85 Fulham Palace Road
London W6 8JB

www.collins.co.uk

Collins is a registered trademark of
HarperCollins Publishers Limited

10 09 08 07 06
6 5 4 3 2 1

A catalogue record for this book is available from
the British Library

Produced for Collins by Essential Works Ltd
168a Camden Street
London NW1 9PT

Editor for Essential Works Ltd: Steve Luck
Designer for Essential Works Ltd: Barbara Doherty
and Michael Gray
Series design: Mark Thomson

ISBN-10: 0-00-724235-2
ISBN-13: 978-0-00-724235-1

Colour reproduction by Colourscan, Singapore
Printed and bound by Printing Express Ltd,
Hong Kong

Contents

Introduction

Believe it or not, if you use the Internet you are in fact already an expert in downloading. Almost everything you do when using the Internet is a form of downloading – whether it's checking your email, browsing webpages or opening attachments. All these actions are a form of downloading.

Similarly, when you put anything onto your computer – be it a digital music track, photos from your digital camera, or an emailed video clip – you're also downloading.

In recent years, the growth both in the number of people downloading material and the amount of material available to download has been startling. Over a decade ago, most files were huge and took hours to download. Today, with faster Internet speeds and enhanced compression technology, it's possible to download almost anything onto your computer quickly and easily – songs, entire music albums, radio shows, short videos, and now even films and television programmes.

At the same time, the scope of what you can do with your downloads is rapidly diversifying. With digital music for example, you can make your own CDs or swap entire tracks with friends via email (as long as you're not breaking any copyright laws). With a portable MP3 player, such as an iPod, you can listen to your entire music collection on the move. Or even fill up your mobile phone with your favourite songs of the moment.

Unfortunately, however, the growing industry in downloading hasn't led to things becoming any easier to understand. The many new types of downloads usually require more than just clicking on a link – you're often expected to download special software and navigate confusing websites.

Need to know? Downloading explains the fundamentals and helps you find and access the best downloads on the Internet. It also shows you what to do with your downloads once you've got them: how to organize, share and make the most of them.

1 Getting started

Nine billion web pages, 160 million music
files, hundreds of video clips - at first glance
the world of downloading from the Internet
seems bewildering. Where do you start? Do
you need any special software? What's the
difference between legal and illegal downloads?
In this opening chapter you'll learn about the
basics of downloading and how to get started
with your first downloads. You'll also learn
how to protect your computer from viruses,
spyware and other dangerous 'malware', so
that you can relax and start enjoying the
adventure of downloading.

The basics of downloading

There are different ways files, whether music, photo or video, can reach your computer. Today, most downloads come from the Internet where there are billions of files to download.

The downloading process

When you download a file, your computer receives the data and stores a copy of it. This process can take seconds or it can take hours – it all depends on the size of the file you're downloading and the speed of your Internet connection.

As recently as five years ago, files on the Internet used to take hours to download. People had slower computers and were predominantly connected to the Internet via modems attached to phone lines. Downloading then was at least ten times slower than using the broadband connections of today.

Technology has now improved and become more widespread, so that everyone can take advantage of this amazing innovation. Today's faster computers have much more storage and bigger hard disks. The Internet is faster all round, and a commercial industry has emerged to supply downloads of music, software, and videos to anyone who wants to download them.

Currently, the most popular form of downloading is music. You can now download almost any track from the world's most popular artists, as well as songs from independent acts, movie sound tracks, radio shows, and audio books. Millions of people around the world are now choosing to download their music rather than buy CDs. And many countries

now even have their own download charts.
Downloading is here to stay.

How big is my download?
Bytes, kilobytes, megabytes, gigabytes – downloads
come in a whole range of sizes; but the jargon used
to describe those sizes can be confusing.

Bytes are the smallest parts of a file; think of them
as letters – A, B, C etc. A kilobyte (Kb) is a thousand
bytes, so think of them as paragraphs. A megabyte
(Mb) is around a thousand kilobytes, so they are
like entire books. Finally, gigabytes are equivalent
to a thousand megabytes so can be thought of as
entire libraries.

You don't necessarily have to remember all that.
Just remember that anything measured in Kbs is
small, Mbs is medium to large, and Gbs is massive.

Here's a guide to how large different types of files
can be and how long they take to download on an
average broadband connection.

type of download	average size	real world	av. download time
documents	5–250Kb	small	seconds
music	1–10Mb	medium	2–10 minutes
software	5–80Mb	medium-large	10–30 minutes
video clips	30–400Mb	large	up to 3 hours
video films	700Mb–1.2Gb	very large	up to 8 hours

Downloading from the web

When you click on a link on a website to download material, the link will usually take you straight to a webpage download. This means the file downloads straight from the computer where the webpage is hosted. This is most common on personal webpages or for very small files such as documents.

Downloading an image

A good example of a common web download is a photograph. Most images on a web page can be downloaded very easily. In fact they are already on your hard-drive; your computer had to download them in order to display the website in your browser. Here we're going to download an image from Flickr, a popular hosting site for photographers.

1 Select the image you want to save. Right click the mouse and choose 'Save Image'. (Mac: CTRL + Click and choose: 'Save Image to the Desktop'.)

2 Save the image file to your desktop or, better still, create a special folder on your computer specially for images and save them there; that way you will easily find them later.

3 To view the saved image, double-click on the file icon or click and drag the image onto your Internet browser and the image will display.

Where's my file?

One of the biggest problems with downloading lots of files is trying to figure out where to put them. Many people just store everything onto their computer's desktop, which then becomes swamped with random files, pictures and documents, making it impossible to find the files you want.

The best thing to do is to create a special folder just for your downloads. Then your files will be easy to find.

Create a download folder

Right click on the desktop (Mac: CTRL + Click). A menu will appear. Select 'Create new folder' (Mac: 'New Folder') and a folder will appear with the name 'New Folder' Type over this name with 'Downloads', and from now on you can save all your downloads into this folder.

Downloading files

The bulk of downloads on the Internet are files. A file can be anything: a song in digital audio format, a document, a video clip or several files in a single file, known as a ZIP or 'archive' file.

must know
Accessing FTP sites
Many public FTP sites allow you to log into them anonymously. Just supply an email address (fake or real) and you can then download what you please. However, other FTP sites may be private and secure (you may have such a site at work or school). If so, you have to obtain a user name and password from the administrator who runs the site before you can access it.

FTP sites and websites

The bulk of files are downloaded not with web downloading but with a method known as FTP (File Transfer Protocol). This may sound technical but it's just a more reliable way of downloading files. If a lot of people are going to download a file, or the file is particularly big, the file is usually stored on a special computer called a file transfer server (FTP server).

What's the difference?

If a website is like a pin board, an FTP site is like a large filing cabinet, containing hundreds of files stored in folders. FTP sites ensure fast downloads that rarely stop or crash. An FTP site is usually stored on large, high-performance computers that can handle thousands of simultaneous downloads without crashing or reducing speeds to a trickle.

Although you can download files from an FTP site using a web browser such as Internet Explorer, downloading in this way is not protected. This means the files are insecure and if the download stops for any reason, you cannot resume from where you left off; you have to start again. However, by using a special FTP program called an FTP client, if your download crashes, you can resume at the point where it broke down, without losing any data.

FTP clients

These let you download multiple files at once, keep track of all your downloads, and allow you to browse the contents of FTP sites. Most have free demo versions you can download and try.

Compressed files

You can download the majority of files on the Internet just by clicking on a link. But often the files you've downloaded are compressed or appear as 'archives'. This means they've been reduced in size so that they download quicker. Several files may be compressed together in this way to make a single smaller file that is easier to download. Either way, this means you have to 'uncompress' them once they're on your computer before you can use them.

The most common form of compressed file is called a ZIP file. On a PC these files have a .ZIP extension on their name instead of say, .TXT for a text file or .DOC for a Word document.

On a Mac, ZIP files have their own icon – a file with a zip on it, no less. ZIP decompressors (or expanders) are built into both PC and Mac operating systems, so opening them is easy. Just double click on the file and it will expand.

However, if you want to control where the resulting file ends up, right-click on the ZIP file and choose 'Expand to ...' and then choose a directory you want the contents to appear in. Unfortunately, you cannot do this on the Mac – uncompressed files always appear in the same directory as the ZIP file.

ZIP

The ZIP icon that appears on Mac computers.

Common problems with downloading

Usually, downloading is a relatively painless affair. Sometimes, however, problems can occur. Here are the most common 'error messages' you might encounter when downloading.

'Error Copying File or Folder' – not enough file space

If your hard disk is full or nearly full, this can often halt a download, especially if you're trying to download a large file. Empty the Recycle Bin (or the waste basket on the Mac). That usually clears some space.

'o% Downloaded'

If the file appears to start downloading but then doesn't progress, the most likely explanation is that the computer at the other end is suffering from bandwidth issues. In other words, too many people may be trying to download the same file at the same time as you. Wait a little while (say 10 minutes). If it doesn't progress, try clicking on the download link again. If it still doesn't work, leave it a couple of hours and then try again. If it still doesn't work, the site or file may be permanently down.

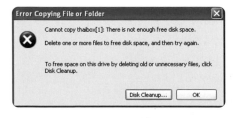

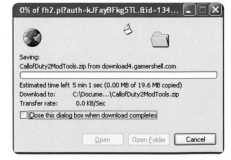

'50% Downloaded'

If your file gets part of the way through the download and freezes, then it's most likely that something has happened to your Internet connection. A lead may inadvertently have been pulled out, your modem may have disconnected, or perhaps your computer has crashed. Check all leads and then restart your computer and try again.

'404 Error' – Page not found

If an error page comes up, this means the file has been removed or is no longer available for some other reason. There's not much you can do at this point other than re-visit the site in the future or use a search engine to find another location for the file.

Garbled characters

If, when you click on a download link, your browser window fills with garbage characters, it means your browser has not recognized the file. Instead of downloading it, it is trying to read it. The best way to get round this is to hold down the ALT key (Mac: Apple key) when you click on the download link and choose 'Save File As ...' from the menu that appears. This will force your browser to download the file.

P2P (peer-to-peer) downloading

A new form of downloading that has arisen in the last five years and become very popular is P2P or 'peer-to-peer' downloading, which is also known as 'file-sharing'. Be wary, however, as there may be legal considerations to take into account.

File-sharing

With P2P, instead of accessing material from one main computer, you download separate small parts of the file from several, sometimes even hundreds of computers simultaneously. These computers are usually owned by other people like you – all downloading and sharing their parts of the same file. This way the file parts are downloaded at the same time and assembled on your computer. No third-party machine or network is needed.

People running the same P2P program can connect with each other and swap and share the files on their hard disks across the Internet. That's why this type of downloading is also known as 'file-sharing'. There are several different types of P2P software. Each uses different language or protocol. Some systems are server-based, which means you log into a network of people using the same program and have access to all their files. In this way you can share files with anyone – and everyone – who's running the same P2P software as you.

watch out!

Because P2P programs are so popular and usually free, the makers sometimes stuff them with spyware – hidden commercial programs that throw adverts and annoying things at you. See page 22 for more information on spyware.

Why P2P?

P2P is a very powerful and robust technology and a great way to download game demos, films, TV and music. Millions of people use the free P2P file-sharing programs to exchange music, videos, software, games and other files over the Internet – and it's a very fast way to download, too.

However, P2P has also become the most popular way to exchange illegal files. Because millions of files are distributed across millions of other computers, it becomes difficult to monitor if any illegal files are exchanged, or even stop them if such files are detected.

Napster was the first popular P2P system and became the most well-known. It was swamped with illegal files and eventually forced to shutdown. Today, though, Napster has been reborn as a legal commercial service for music downloads. In its stead, names like BitTorrent, Kazaa and eMule now rule the P2P universe.

Popular P2P programs

There are many different networks out there and many different types of software for P2P file-sharing. Many require you to share your files as well as downloading others. The number of users and files available varies from system to system.

BitTorrent (Mac and PC)

This is currently the biggest P2P program and generally regarded as the best. Torrent files can be found on webpages all over the Internet. Clicking on links on the sites launches BitTorrent, which then handles the downloads for you. It's an extremely efficient way of obtaining files. There are many different programs that offer interfaces and 'front-ends' for BitTorrent to make it easier to use. They're worth rooting out, and can be found at www.bittorrent.com/

Kazaa (PC)

Once the most popular file-sharing program, Kazaa is now declining in popularity. It suffers from a great deal of spyware (see page 22), and its network is full of illegal and fake files. Avoid. www.kazaa.com/us/index.htm

eDonkey (PC / Mac)

A very popular network and program, especially in Europe, eDonkey is quite technical to install and use but has millions of users and thousands of servers, swapping mostly illegal files. The free version has built-in adverts but no spyware. www.edonkey2000.com/

Acquisition (Mac only)

This is a Mac only program and has a very clean, easy-to-use interface. It spans several popular file-sharing networks such as BitTorrent and Limewire and works directly with iPod and iTunes. www.acquisitionx.com/

Limewire (Mac and PC)

Very popular, clean and easy-to-use, Limewire is a well-established program that connects across a massive P2P network known as Gnutella. It is also spyware- and advert-free. Worth taking a look. www.limewire.com/english/content/home.html

Legality warning!

Most P2P downloading networks are hubs for illegal downloads. Illegal downloads are a big problem on the Internet. People exchange pirated albums, files and software programs in their millions every day. It's often hard to tell what's legal and what's not. A good rule of thumb is if you're downloading using a P2P program and you're not sure whether a file is legal, it's probably not. So it's probably best not to download it.

Safe downloading

While the Internet has improved our lives and created an incredible array of new tools, it's also created many nasty inventions. Trojans, spyware, malware, spam relays, viruses – these are all 'malware', software designed to infect your computer and disrupt your files.

Security

The Internet makes it incredibly easy to exchange information all over the world. But that openness and power also make it easy for hackers and criminals to exploit the network. Some 'malware' may even secretly commandeer your Internet connection for dangerous or nefarious means.

Most hackers are young and out to cause mischief, more for sport than any criminal gain. But some are 'cyber-criminals' and would not think twice about lifting your credit card details or important passwords from your computer.

Today's Internet is awash with various different types of malicious programs designed to attach themselves to unprotected computers and wreak havoc. The most common way for such programs to become installed on a computer is hidden in downloaded files. If you do not have anti-virus software installed, your computer is almost certain to become infected.

The good news is that this threat is very easy to protect against. All you need is a basic understanding of the threat and a few (mostly free) pieces of software to secure your computer against infection.

Viruses, Trojans and worms

These small programs are the most common type of 'malware'. They're designed to infiltrate computers and networks by making copies of themselves and spreading via emails, CDs, and downloadable files. Some viruses are harmless and do nothing other than spread themselves. Others are malicious and may delete data such as emails and documents. In the worst cases, they can crash your computer and erase your hard disk.

Spyware

Spyware is often hidden in free programs down-loaded from the web. Once installed, the spyware gathers information on the websites you browse and the words you use in search engines and secretly transmits that information to advertisers. The advertisers then send you banners and 'pop-up' ads you don't want or change your web browser's settings so you always end up at their sites. Very malicious spyware may log your keystrokes in an attempt to obtain your passwords.

Protecting your computer

It's essential these days to install some form of protection for your computer, especially if you're downloading. Anything could get in. The best way to secure your machine is to install several layers of protection.

Anti-virus programs

These essential programs scan all files coming into your computer – via email, CD, or the Internet. If they find a virus or other 'malware', they alert you and delete it. They can also periodically scan your entire computer for files. It's good practice to perform this kind of scan once a week.

must know

Attachments:
Viruses like to hide inside files as attachments to emails. As a rule, don't open an attachment in an email unless you are 100% certain it is safe. Many modern viruses disguise themselves inside emails that look convincingly like error messages or emails from your bank or IT support department. The safest thing to do is to always scan the email attachment with an anti-virus program before you open it.

watch out!

Symptoms of a malware infected computer:
• starts running slowly
• shuts off unexpectedly or crashes a lot
• 'memory errors'
• unusual files or folders appear
• strange messages or adverts appear

We recommend:

Norton Antivirus – www.symantec.com/index.htm

McAfee Antivirus – www.mcafee.com/

Firewall

A firewall is a software program that blocks unauthorized users from accessing your computer. Think of it as a policeman, blocking any traffic you didn't specifically ask for from your computer. It also stops you if any programs on your computer try to access the Internet without your permission. Some anti-virus programs also include firewall support.

We recommend:

F-Secure Internet Security – www.f-secure.com/

Kapersky Internet Security – www.kaspersky.com/

Little Snitch – www.obdev.at/products/littlesnitch/index.html (Mac)

Anti-spyware

Similar to anti-virus programs, anti-spyware will scan your computer periodically to find and delete any spyware. Such programs, however, have to be kept up-to-date as new types of spyware appear everyday on the Internet.

We recommend:

Microsoft Windows Defender – www.microsoft.com/athome/security/spyware/software/default.mspx

Lavasoft Ad-Aware SE – www.lavasoft.de/software/adaware/

Spybot Search & Destroy – www.safer-networking.org/

want to know more?
• See pages 24-47 to find out about what files to download.

• Try downloading a free FTP client to help you download multiple files, keep track of all your downloads and allow you to browse FTP sites.

• Note that when 'ftp://' instead of 'http://' appears in your browser, that means you are looking at an FTP site, not a website.

weblinks
• FTP clients for PCs: www.cuteftp.com/ www.smartftp.com/
• FTP clients for Macs www.panic.com/transmit/ www.fetchsoftworks.com/
• Visit www.microsoft.com/security to find out about the latest Windows malware protection.

2 What to download

There have never been so many files to download from the Internet – and what a selection. Every day, thousands of new music tracks, video clips, games demos and software programs are added to the millions already on the web, collectively creating confusing arrays of file formats and options. In this chapter, we take you through the most popular downloads. We'll show you what you need to get started and where to start looking to find the latest and best downloads. We'll also show you how to obtain updates for your computer so it stays in good shape and free from viruses and spam.

Downloading music

The music industry is currently undergoing a revolution. Slowly but inevitably CDs are going out of fashion. In their place there are high-quality digital music files, downloadable from the Internet whenever you want.

Online music stores

A new breed of online record shops is replacing the traditional high street store. The biggest online music outlet – Apple's iTunes Music Store – boasts well over two million tracks. To date, over a billion songs have already been downloaded from this site since its launch in 2003.

Apple's store is being joined online by an increasing number of rivals. Among them are Napster, Rhapsody and AOL Music – all massive music stores offering millions of songs to browse, buy and download. At the same time, thousands of unsigned artists and bubbling-under bands are promoting their music for free online. And even commercial artists are offering free downloads, rarities and B-sides on their own websites.

These online music stores and outlets work just like interactive catalogues. Just choose the song you want, perhaps listen to a short preview, and then download it onto your hard drive and listen to it immediately. It's easy, legal and (relatively) inexpensive.

must know

If you connect to the Internet via 'dial-up', you can still download music but individual tracks are going to take at least ten minutes to download.

The big plus with downloading music is that once you've downloaded a file you can do almost anything you like with it. It's yours. You can store it for long periods of time, copy it onto other computers or portable devices, burn it onto a CD, or give it to other people.

What you need to download music

Most modern computers are more than able to handle digital music. Here's what you need:

- PC or Mac computer – the faster the processor and the bigger the hard disk, the better
- a credit card – for buying songs online or subscribing to online stores
- lots of disk space – for storing tracks (the average three-minute track weighs in at around 3 Mb)
- sound card – to connect to your amp and speakers so you can hear your downloaded music
- player program – to act as a jukebox to collect and organize your downloads
- a fast (broadband) Internet connection – to download your tracks

File formats

Although actually downloading music is simple, the vast range of different music file formats can be confusing.

In their raw form, digital music files are much too big to be easily downloaded from the Internet. Because of this all downloadable music has to be compressed, usually to about a tenth or thereabouts of its original size, to make it accessible on the Internet. Luckily, this is usually managed without any noticeable loss in quality.

There are several different ways of compressing music, unfortunately. Each has been developed by a different company or group over years, leading to today's messy file format salad.

The most common format is the MP3 format, which is used all over the Internet today. It's the CD of the digital music world and everyone uses it. Many portable players are called MP3 players and every computer and player today will play these files.

Some of the other formats – such as Windows Media Audio (WMA) and Apple's AAC format – provide better sound quality than the MP3 format, but are larger and require more storage space. Others create smaller files than the MP3 format and are best suited for portable music players such as the iPod.

MP3 stands for MPEG-1 Audio Layer 3 and the files can be recognized by the extension '.mp3'. Most digital audio is available in MP3 format. The sound quality is very good and it achieves its small file size by stripping out sound frequencies the human ear cannot detect.

AAC is Apple's proprietary format and is generally considered to provide better quality than MP3. Apple's iTunes player, its music store and the iPod all use AAC by default (although they will also support the MP3 format). To make things more complicated, some PC-compatible music players will not play AAC.

WMA stands for Windows Media Audio, and is Microsoft's answer to the MP3 file. WMA files are good quality and are noticeably smaller than MP3 files. It is a very popular format online and for portable music players. Watch out though – Apple's iTunes player and the iPod will not play them. They have to be converted, one by one, into AAC files.

must know

On the Internet, music is split into files that you can download and files that can be 'streamed'. 'Streaming' means audio you listen to 'live' while you're connected to the Internet. Think of it as having music 'transmitted' to you like a TV program rather than downloading it. Your computer receives it, you listen to it, but you don't get to keep a copy. Music sites often stream sections or tracks for free. Others charge a small fee to listen to the stream.

WAV is an uncompressed PC format which means the quality is very high, as good as a CD. However, the file size is huge (10 Mbs per minute) so it's impractical for Internet use. While some online stores allow you to download using this format, it's mainly used for sound recording and radio production.

AIFF (Audio Interchange File Format) is an uncompressed Mac format. Like WAV files, these are high quality but cripplingly large in size. Like WAVs, they are used in audio production and when recording and editing radio programs such as podcasts (see pages 156 75).

Legality warning

Illegal music downloading has dominated the Internet music scene for years. So much so that it's sometimes difficult to tell whether the website you're downloading from is legitimate or not. Add to that the various different types of copy protection (or 'Digital Rights Management') the stores add to their download, and you can sometimes be forgiven for the feeling that you're accidentally breaking the law somehow if you burn a track onto a CD or download an MP3 file for a friend.

Generally, it's acceptable to download tracks from a popular branded store – like iTunes, Rhapsody or Napster. Burning them onto CDs for your own personal use is also okay. If you start handing them out to your friends, you're probably breaking the law, but you won't be arrested. If you're sharing your downloaded tracks – or any copyright tracks or files – on a P2P system, then you're definitely breaking the law. And you could be prosecuted for it.

Download a free track from iTunes Music Store

1 Click on the green 'Music Store' icon in the left-hand iTunes window. The store will load in the iTunes window much like a website.

2 Amid the rows of icons, in the middle of the featured artists' slot, you should see an icon labelled 'Free Download Of The Week'. Click on it.

3 You'll find yourself on the 'Single Of The Week' screen. Below the image, you'll see a list of free tracks available to download.

4 For a 30-second preview, double-click on the title. There may be a delay before it starts (depending on your Internet connection).

watch out!

Few songs are free at the iTunes store. You'll be paying for your downloads. It's easy to forget that until you get your credit card bill! See page 80-81 for tips on saving money on digital music.

5 Click on 'Get Song'. A screen will appear prompting you to log in or sign up for a new account. If you already have an account you can enter your password here. If not, you'll need to sign up for an account.

6 Once you're logged in, iTunes will prompt you one final time to ensure you really want to download your selected song. Answer Yes and the song will download onto your computer for free.

7 You'll find your latest download in the Purchased Music folder in the left hand window. Listen to it, copy it – do whatever you like, it's yours.

Apple's iTunes store currently offers more music than any other site – all of which you can download for a reasonable fee. One catch: you need the free iTunes audio player to use it. Download iTunes at: www.apple.com/itunes and see our guide to using iTunes on pages 53-6.

must know

Each song you download from the iTunes Music Store can be copied to five other computers, excluding your iPod, but no more. So, for example, you can have a copy on your main computer, and one on your laptop, and perhaps one on your computer at work. Each track must be authorized however, which means you need to enter your iTunes password the first time you play it on the new machine.

Downloading video

Right now, downloadable video is exploding on the Internet – there's so much to see. You can watch breaking news, download trailers of the latest film releases, buy episodes of your favourite TV shows and much much more. We're going to teach you how to access all this with just a few clicks.

must know

AVI videos can also use different types of compression to get the best results. However, this means sometimes you may download a file that uses a compressor you don't have on your computer. You can download all the current ones from here: www.download.com/A VI-Codec-Pack/3000- 2169_410391962. html and www.microsoft.com /windows/windowsme dia/player/faq/ codec.mspx

It's easy

Now you can download video as easily as you can download music. And, as with digital music, once you download video clips or episodes, they're yours. You can treat them just like a file on your computer and do with them as you wish. Make copies and move them around your computer? No problem. Burn them onto CDs or load them onto other computers at home? Easy. Download them onto your iPod or other portable player and watch them on the move? Effortless.

What's available?

Downloadable video online is split into two categories – pay and free. Free clips include film trailers, news broadcasts, music video, and millions of odd and interesting home-made clips Internet users have uploaded to sites like Google Video.

Pay video works very much in the same way as the downloadable music market, but is currently a lot smaller. This is due partly to the sheer size of video files – they can be anything from between ten and a hundred times larger than music files.

Another reason online video is so scarce is that TV and film companies are unsure about how they want to sell their products online and what to do about copyright issues. For these reasons big companies are being very tentative about their shows being available on the Internet.

However, in the US you can already download the latest episodes of top-rated TV shows from sites such as the iTunes Music Store for a fee. You can even opt to download iPod-ready versions to watch on the move. In the UK, the BBC are readying themselves to make a lot of their programming available on the Internet. It won't be long now before most TV programmes and even movie blockbusters will be available on demand to download from the web.

The quality

While online videos these days are mostly of a good quality, some are not – it usually depends on where you're downloading from. While not as vivid or as detailed as DVD video, downloaded commercial video is usually of a very high quality and very watchable, with barely any 'artefacts' or 'drop outs' – as problems in digital video are called.

This image shows how a video image degrades the more you compress it.

In comparison, however, home-made clips or streaming video from a news website can be of an inferior quality: with skipping frames, blurry visuals, and juddering action. There are ways to get round this however. See our page on Streaming Video (page 39) for more detail.

What you need to download video

Downloading and watching digital videos require a little more from your computer than downloading music does. The list on the next page explains what you need.

- PC or a Mac computer with a fast processor to guarantee smooth playback
- large hard disk with lots of disk space – for storing downloaded videos, which can take up as much as 10 Mbs a minute
- sound card – to connect to your amp and speakers so you can hear the sound track
- player program – such as Windows Media Player or iTunes to play your downloaded videos
- a fast (broadband) Internet connection – if you connect to the Internet through your phone line, it's going to be too slow for downloading most videos. Sorry, this is a broadband-only hobby

Different video formats

As with music downloads, there are a selection of different video file formats available online, each with its own strengths and weaknesses. In its raw format, digital video is far too large to share over the Internet, so various compression formats have been developed to reduce files to more download-friendly sizes.

AVI is an abbreviation for Audio Video Interleaved. This Microsoft format is the oldest and most common video format. It provides good quality, is flexible, and will play on most PCs and Macs.

WMV stands for Windows Media Video. It is the latest video format from Microsoft. It provides very high-quality visuals and sound. Today's video sellers and download sites usually have WMV versions of their films to download.

try this

To watch AVI movies on the Mac, download the free VLC (VideoLAN Client) player. Go to: www.videolan.org/vlc/download-macosx.html

QuickTime is Apple's video format and one of the most popular. It typically offers very high-quality images and sound, right up to cinema quality if your computer is powerful enough. QuickTime movies will play without any problem on Apple Mac computers, but PC owners will have to download the PC version of Quicktime for free. www.apple.com/quicktime/download/win.html

DivX is an independent format, not developed by commercial companies. It is worth mentioning here as it is very popular online, of a very high quality, and free. We highly recommend downloading it: www.divx.com

MPEG stands for Motion Picture Experts Group. MPEG videos are identified by the .MPG or .MPEG suffix at the end of the file names. There are several different versions of MPEG video, with picture quality varying from low to stunning.
MPEG-1 the oldest version, low quality but good enough for small, short clips
MPEG-2 the high-quality version, used to fit movies onto DVDs
MPEG-4 very high quality with relatively small file sizes for Internet and iPod use.

Real Video is a very common format and one you'll see almost everywhere on the Internet. However, the Real format (also known as RealVideo or RealPlayer-compatible) is designed primarily for streaming video, in other words video you receive on your computer similar to a TV transmission, but one that you cannot download and keep. See Streaming Music and Video on pages 39-41 to learn more.

In addition, you may also come across video in Xvid format. This is a free open-source version of Xvid, which offers the same quality as DivX.

Download video for free

The bulk of video on the Internet is currently free, but it won't be like that for much longer. As long as you've got enough disk space and plenty of time to explore, you can dig up some real gems without spending a penny.

Viewing videos

You can choose three different formats for your video. To watch it on your computer, choose 'Windows/Mac'. If you're planning to view the clip on your iPod or Playstation Portable, you can download films that are the correct size and format for those players – just choose the appropriate option from the pull-down menu before you hit 'download'.

One of the most popular things to download online are film trailers. Teasers, extended trailers and other exciting previews for big films are now released on the web before anywhere else, and the quality is often stunning. Visit www.apple.com/trailers and start downloading.

Many trailers and video downloads – and all iPod downloads – on the Internet use QuickTime format. Unfortunately this format is not built into Windows. So to watch these clips, you'll have to download the QuickTime software free from: www.apple.com/quicktime.

try this

Google make their own video player program, custom-designed to work seamlessly with their website. Download it from: http:// video.google.com

Google Video

The search engine giant's video outlet is tremendous fun. It's full of wacky home clips, ancient and exotic documentaries, music videos, and a bizarre range of uncategorizable clips. Best of all, every clip is free to download. Visit http://video.google.com and follow these steps:

1 Google Video uses a very simple interface designed in the same way as its search engine. Just click on the pictures or menus to instantly watch the clips.

2 On the top navigation bar, click on Google Picks to see a 'best of' Google video gallery. Scroll through the selection and click on a clip you like the look of.

3 On this screen, depending on how your computer is set up, you may see a blank screen or the video may start immediately.

4 If it's playing, click on the play button to stop playback. Instead click on the download button in the right-hand column.

5 The download should begin automatically and the file should download to your desktop. Double-click on the clip to watch it.

2 What to download

Download film trailers for your iPod

1 Browse Apple's trailers' site, which lists all the downloads for current and forthcoming films. Clips labelled HD (High Definition) are ultra-high quality.

2 Click on the title of a film and you'll be taken to its home page. Here you can decide on the size of your download. Once you've selected the size, select 'Download for iPod'.

3 The file will start downloading. iPod trailers are usually compressed in ZIP files to make them quicker to download (see page 15).

4 Once it's downloaded, the file will probably 'unpack' (decompress) itself. If it doesn't you can easily unpack it yourself by double-clicking its icon on the desktop.

5 Double-click on it again to watch the clip in iTunes. From here you can also transfer the clip straight to your iPod.

Streaming music and video

Streaming is an alternative to downloading. Like a TV station broadcasting a programme to your TV, a website can transmit or stream video to your computer, and it has many advantages. Streaming is great for live webcasts for example, but it has one downside – you don't get to keep a copy of the video!

Listening online

Despite the growing trend for downloading anything and everything, streaming is still very popular. Many radio shows and podcasts (subscription radio) use streaming audio. You choose broadcasts by genre – jazz, classical or indie – and listen to radio stations all over the world. Some broadcasters like the BBC stream their entire radio output online. All webcasts of concerts, interviews and news events use streaming video to broadcast the pictures to thousands of people watching on the Internet.

When you're shopping, streaming is good because you can quickly tell whether you like something or not, without having to sit and wait for the whole file to download. But unlike downloading, you don't retain a copy of what you're watching or listening to. You have to keep visiting the site to hear the track. Commercial Internet broadcasters use this to retain copyright over their recordings.

What's the quality like?

The quality of streaming video depends on the speed and stability of your Internet connection – the faster the connection, the better the picture and sound quality. If your connection goes slow for a moment, a

The quality of streamed video varies depending on the speed of your internet connection.

video or audio webcast will automatically drop the quality to keep the connection going rather than cut you off. Overall, though, it's more than acceptable most of the time.

Popular formats

As with downloadable video, various different video streaming formats have emerged over the years.

RealAudio

RealAudio is the longest-standing and most popular form of streaming audio and video. Although the BBC and other broadcasters utilize the format, it has become less popular in recent years thanks to competition from rivals. Picture quality is quite good and scaleable, which means you can watch video even on the slowest Internet connections. Download the free player at: www.real.com/player/

QuickTime

For extremely high-quality streaming audio, most websites choose QuickTime. Nearly all film trailers are in QuickTime format and many pop videos go the same route to maintain quality. PC users need to download and install the free QuickTime software to use this method of streaming: www.apple.com/quicktime

Flash

Flash is a common add-on for web browser programs to display animations on webpages. It also supports video and audio streaming. Many of the leading websites now use Flash to supply streams to their visitors. Download the latest free player from: www.macromedia.com/flash

Troubleshooting streaming

Because streaming video is quite an intensive task for your computer to perform, things can sometimes go wrong. Here's a list of common problems:

Nothing happens

There is often an initial waiting period as the stream fills up your player. Players often 'read ahead' to make sure they can play continuously. This is known as 'buffering'. Once the player's buffer is filled with around four or five seconds of material, it begins playing. If nothing happens after 60 seconds, try re-clicking on the link.

Stream stutters or stops

This usually indicates a bandwidth issue – the stream is being interrupted either because a lot of people are trying to access the same file simultaneously, or something on your computer is stealing the bandwidth. Check to see if any other programs are downloading. Restarting the stream usually helps.

Quality drops

If the music you're listening to suddenly sounds low-quality, tinny or switches from stereo to mono, it usually means that the bandwidth available has dropped for some reason and the server is trying to keep your streaming connection by dropping the quality. Drops in quality are usually temporary, and it's likely that the quality will improve after a short period of time.

www.bbc.co.uk/radio will bring up a list of all BBC radio stations.

Choose a station you like and then click on 'Listen Live' in the top right of the screen.

The BBC Radio Player will appear.

Listening to radio

The Internet has several great radio stations you can listen to for free 24 hours day. Some are web versions of existing FM stations, others stream exclusive Internet-only content. The two main players – iTunes and Windows Media Player – both have support for radio built-in to the program, ensuring that listening couldn't be easier.

If you cannot hear any sound or the radio player doesn't seem to be working, it could mean you don't have the correct RealPlayer software installed. Visit www.real.com/player/ and select 'Free Player' to download this.

Windows Media Player

Ensure you are connected to the Internet and then click on the 'Guide' tab on the top taskbar. Then select 'Radio Tuner' on the webpage that opens. A list of radio stations will appear.

iTunes

In the left-hand 'Source' pane is an icon labelled 'Radio'. Click on this to bring up a list of stations currently playing. Double-click on the station name to start listening.

Downloading software

Apart from music and video, the Internet is also a rich source of software – programs that you can run on your computer. Here we take you through the basics of finding and downloading the best software for your computer.

What's available

Whatever you may want or need for your computer, the Internet is likely to have it. Utilities, audio and video players, security software such as anti-virus programs, design packages, productivity packages and essential patches and updates to keep your computer's operating system in excellent condition.

A lot of software is free. For example, Apple's iTunes or Microsoft's Media Player are free to download and keep. At the same time, you can download free trial or demo versions for most software and games. Many fully-functioning trial versions will run for 30 days, while stripped-down demo versions of software will often work indefinitely.

Where to find software

Several large sites on the Internet form the hub of a vast download library. A lot of software is below par so many of these sites review the programs they host in order to ensure quality. Look out for:

www.download.com
All the software you could possibly want.
www.fileplanet.com/
Downloads and game demos for a younger audience.
www.apple.com/downloads/macosx/
The latest and best Apple software.

must know

The best way for a virus or similar piece of 'malware' to find its way onto your computer is through a downloaded program. Audio and video are relatively safe in this regard, but applications, demos and games are not. See pages 21–3 on Safe Downloading to learn how to secure your computer.

Updating your operating system (Windows)

1 Visit the Microsoft Update page at http://update.microsoft.com/microsoftupdate and click on 'Start Now'.

2 Follow the onscreen instructions and click on 'Install' to download and run the update software.

3 Next, click on 'Turn it On Now' and then 'Change Settings' to turn on automatic updates in the future.

4 Now select 'Check For Updates', followed by 'Express Updates'. This will scan your computer for the essential updates it needs.

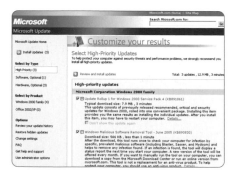

5 Sit back and wait while they download.

Updating Your Operating System (Mac OS)

1 Under the Apple menu, choose the 'Software Update' option.

2 Your computer will start searching for new software. (This can take a few minutes.)

3 A list appears of all the latest updates. A blue arrow alongside a file name means that the computer will have to restart if you download it. Click on the title of the update to read the details.

4 Tick the updates you want to install and click on the 'Install' button.

5 An automated process will take over. The patch will be downloaded and the computer will restart and refresh itself automatically.

Other downloads

Other than music, videos, and documents, there are various innovative and sometimes highly unusual files to download for help and information. If you're interested in exploring, try these:

Tours & Maps

If you're into travelling, you can download a whole range of guides to foreign cities and interesting cultural spaces such as museums and art galleries. These come in various forms: interactive maps, video guides and audio commentaries. Most are fully compatible with iPods and other players so you can listen (and view) while on the move. PodGuides – www.podguides.net

Audio Books

All kinds of books – popular, fiction and non-fiction – now come in audio-only versions. They're sold alongside their paper counterparts on sites like

Amazon, but increasingly they're becoming a popular feature of online music stores like the iTunes Music Store and Audible.
Audible.com – www.audible.com

eBooks

Fully electronic books were once touted to replace the traditional printed book, but they have never really caught on. Nevertheless, in recent years, cheaper printers and laptops have made these downloadable books a more viable concept. Cookbooks, self-help and study guides have proven very popular.
Download free eBooks at Manybooks: www.manybooks.net

3 Digital music

Now that you've learned how to download various types of media, it's likely that you will soon have a range of different file types sitting on your computer. The chances are the bulk of those will be digital music files. In this chapter the basics of digital music are explained – how to listen to it and how to organize it using the powerful digital music player software that comes with your computer or which is readily available to be downloaded. Here we will also show you how to copy tracks onto portable players, such as an iPod, so that you can listen to your music wherever you are.

Digital music players

At the heart of your download collection sits your player – hi-fi, jukebox and CD-maker all in one. We'll be looking at the two most popular players – Windows Media Player and iTunes.

try this

Often the Windows Media Player can dominate the screen and get in the way of anything you're doing. If so, shrink it. On your desktop, right-click on the bar at the bottom of the screen, known as the taskbar. Click on an area without anything in it (next to the clock is good). From the menu that appears, select 'Toolbars' and then 'Windows Media Player'. This sets up Windows Media Player to minimize (flip to small mode) on the task bar.

Home entertainment

Your digital music player can do everything a hi-fi can do and much more. It really is a complete home entertainment system. Not only will it scoop up all your digital music into a single, easy-to-manage collection, it will also play videos, receive radio broadcasts, and enable you to shop for downloads online. It will even put on a light show if you know how to ask.

Windows Media Player and iTunes are made by Microsoft and Apple respectively. Both are free and both have similar features and capabilities. There are, however, some slight differences. Over the next few pages we'll be taking you on a detailed tour of both.

Windows Media Player (WMP)

Windows Media Player (WMP) is Microsoft's flagship digital player and is, more often than not, preloaded onto just about every recent PC. With WMP you can browse your music files, copy tracks to portable players and burn CDs. You can also use it to go online and buy music.

Warning: WMP only runs on Windows PCs and will not work with iPods.

1 These tabs along the top allow you to switch between WMP main modes

2 *Now Playing* is the track playlists or videos currently racked up to play

3 *Library* allows you to see all your tracks listed

4 *Rip* is for digitizing tracks from audio CDs (see page 84)

5 *Burn* is the page where you can make your own CDs

6 *Sync* is for transferring (or 'synchronizing') music tracks onto your portable player

7 *Guide* gives you access to online downloads

8 The main library screen lists the artist's name and the title of the track

9 Extra information about the playlist you're playing can be found here

10 *Now Playing List* – drag tracks here to stack them up for listening

11 *The play bar* – here you can control playback of your tracks. The green bar at the bottom shows how far the track currently playing has progressed

12 *Playlist window* – this area contains all the different lists of music you have made or your computer has auto-generated

13 *All Music* – click this to see all the music Windows Media Player can find on your computer

14 *Playlists* – click on these to expand and reveal the contents

15 *Online Stores* – this leads to various online media outlets where you can download music (see Chapter 4, Buying music online)

Using the graphic equalizer in Windows Media Player

1 In the 'Now Playing' window, click on the downwards-pointing arrow icon in the top left-hand corner.

2 Under the 'Enhancement' menu, select 'Graphic Equalizer'.

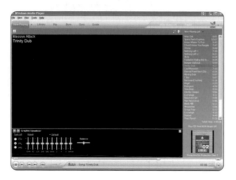

3 A graphic equalizer panel will appear underneath the main window.

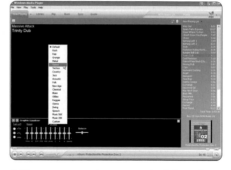

4 There are several presets ranked along the left. Click the buttons alongside them to activate them. Or, you can click and drag the various sliders with the mouse. If you want to reset the graphic equalizer, click on the word 'Default' just above the graphic equalizer bars.

try this

Click the blue left and right arrows in the EQ pan to explore the other enhancements.

Playing music with iTunes

iTunes is the only player that fully works with the iPod. It is well designed and has a host of excellent features and little touches that make it a joy to use. While it works on both Macs and PCs, unfortunately, the only player it works with directly is the iPod.

1 The *Library* is all your music, unsorted, unfiltered, organized into columns such as name, artist, album and so on. To play a song just double-click the name in the main window

2 *Podcasts* hosts all Internet radio shows you have subscribed to and perhaps downloaded

3 *Videos* contains any video clips you've downloaded or imported into iTunes

4 *Party Shuffle* is a special kind of playlist (see page 116 for details)

5 *Music Store* is a direct link to the iTunes Apple Store

6 *Audio CD* – if you have a music CD inserted in your computer, it will appear here

7 *'Source'* window contains a list of the various ways iTunes can gather your music

8 Skip tracks with the left and right buttons.

9 Volume slider allows you to control the playback volume

10 Status Display shows the current track playing, the artist who recorded it, and the time remaining on the track

11 Purple icons like these represent 'Smart Playlists', which are themed lists of songs generated from your music collection

12 Blue icons represent the playlists you've created

13 *Icon Shelf* (from left to right) loads the iTunes Music Store into a mini window; turns on the graphic equalizer; turns on Visuals (see page 113), ejects a CD (if you have a CD in your computer)

Accessing the graphic equalizer in iTunes

1 Click on the graphic equalizer icon on the lower right corner of the iTunes main screen.

2 On the graphic equalizer window, tick the blue box in the top left corner to activate it.

try this

To save space on screen switch iTunes to 'minimode'. On a PC, under the 'Advanced' menu, choose 'Switch To Mini Player'. On a Mac, click on the green plus (+) sign in the top left of the iTunes window to toggle between mini and full modes.

3 Move the preamp slider to boost the overall volume of the output.

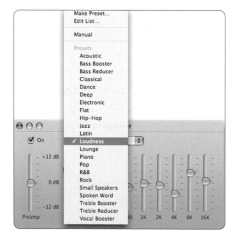

4 Unless you're a hi-fi aficionado, you're better off just using the presets. Access these by clicking on the menu above the sliders.

Player basics

Some quick tips to get you started with your digital player. Once you've mastered these basics, you'll be ready for more advanced tips on page 83.

Advanced playing

The Shuffle button will ensure a random track is chosen next. By clicking on the button repeatedly you can cycle through the various options. Repeat Song, as it sounds, will repeat the track over and over again until you unclick it.

Finding a song

Once you start building up your collection of music, finding specific songs quickly will become more of a problem. The two programs – iTunes and Windows Media Player – search slightly differently.

iTunes

In the upper right corner of the iTunes window is a search field with a magnifying glass in it. Just start typing the name of the song, artist, or album, and as you start typing iTunes will immediately start searching and displaying the matches it's found in the main window. If you want to clear the search results, just click on the grey and white 'x' in the corner of the search box.

Windows Media Player

Flip to the Library view, and type in your song name, artist, or other search term into the search box in the top right-hand corner. Hit the Return key to begin the search.

Deleting a song

If you decide a song is not worthy of being in your collection or on a playlist, you can remove it in a second by pressing Delete (or backspace on the Mac). Depending on what you're doing, two things will happen. If you're playing from within a playlist, the song will be removed from that playlist, but not deleted from your collection. If you're in the Library view, iTunes will move the file to the wastebin (with your permission of course).

You can delete a block of multiple tracks at the same time by holding down the Shift key, selecting the first track and then the last track. All the tracks in-between will be highlighted. Hit Delete and they'll all be sent to the wastebin.

Changing the sort order

You can see that different columns in iTunes give different information: name, time, artist, album and so on. Clicking in one of the columns will resort the list based on that category. For example, clicking on genre will organize the songs alphabetically by genre. You can do this with any column. Useful sort categories include 'Date added' and 'My rating'.

Finding the song playing

iTunes

Often when you're playing a song, you may well be browsing Apple's Music Store or checking out other playlists on your computer at the same time. Suddenly you may find that you cannot get back to the track or playlist you're playing. Simply press Apple + L and you'll be instantly transported to the song that's playing – no matter where you are.

Windows Media Player

In Windows Media Player there are two ways to return to the song that's playing. Either click the large 'Now Playing' tag, or the 'Now Playing' link running down the side.

Burning music on CD

Digital music you've downloaded is fantastically easy to copy or 'burn' onto CD. You can make compilations and burn entire albums from the music in your collection and then play them in your stereo or car.

What software?

You don't need extra software to burn CDs. You can do it right now. The digital music players in this chapter – Windows Media Player and iTunes – both allow you to make an unlimited amount of CDs anytime you want. Best of all, it's quick. You can usually burn a CD in under ten minutes!

What media?

You'll need some blank recordable CDs, also known as CD-Rs. These are usually very cheap to buy and come in bundles of ten or more. Each disk can store a maximum of 74 minutes of music – that's about 20 songs.

Both programs will also print CD inserts (with graphics if you want) so you can have some good-looking inlays for your homemade CDs.

must know

You can burn audio tracks on Rewriteable CDs (CD-RWs) - CDs that allow you to record on them over and over again. However, many stereos and CD players will not play CD-RWs, so it's best to stick with less expensive CD-Rs.

3 Digital music

Burn a CD in Windows Media Player

1 Open Windows Media Player and select 'Library' and choose 'Burn List' from the 'Now Playing' menu at the top of the screen.

2 Drag folders, playlist, or individual tracks into the 'Burn List' to create a track listing for your CD.

3 Insert a blank CD-R into your computer.

4 Move songs around and change their order if you like. But keep an eye on the Total Time display at the bottom. Make sure it doesn't go over 1:14:00.

5 To start copying files to the CD, click the 'Start Burn' arrow and choose 'Audio CD' from the menu that appears. Once the CD is burned, it will appear in the contents pane on the left of the screen.

Burn a CD in iTunes

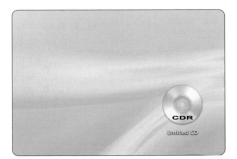

1 Open iTunes and insert a blank CD-R into your computer.

2 Select a playlist you want to copy to CD. Drag the songs around if you like to change the order. See page 93 to learn how to create a playlist if you're unsure

3 Check the playing length of the playlist to make sure it's no more than 74 minutes.

4 Click the 'Burn' button in the top right corner and start the copying process.

5 Once the files are copied, a CD icon will appear in the 'Source List' on the left-hand side. Click the small grey 'Eject' button next to the CD name to eject the CD.

On the move

Without a doubt the greatest innovation in the digital music arena is the invention of the portable player. Portable music devices, such as Sony's Walkman, minidisc players, and portable CD players, have existed for some time – but never before have they been able to hold so much music or been so flexible.

Portable players

With your portable player you can do much more than play music. You can listen to radio shows on the move, browse pictures, watch films and music videos, or even your favourite TV shows.

There are many players on the market – in fact, the choice is bewildering. There are the market leaders and the clones of the market leaders. Apple's iPod dominates, of course, and most people opt for this stylish and powerful player, although many of its rival players are also worth considering.

How to choose a player

Very little distinguishes players in terms of sound quality – they all sound great. That's the power of digital music. At the same time, because the market is so competitive, there's also little to differentiate them in terms of price and features – many offer the same storage capacities and battery life, for example. When investing in a digital music player, one question to ask

watch out

Not all portable players use replaceable batteries. Most notorious is the iPod, which you have to return to Apple if the battery dies. And of course there's a fee to replace it.

must know

Be warned. Your new pride and joy will get scratched. Coffee will be spilt. You will drop it. More than likely food will get worked into the controls. It's advisable to protect your player from the elements right from the start. There are a broad range of cases, pouches and socks available for digital players – buy one at the same time you buy your player; you won't regret it.

yourself is what you will use it for. Obviously you'll want to listen to music, but how much music? If you've got a small record collection, you may not need a player with a massive 10 Gb or more storage space. And will you want to load it up with photos? Do you see yourself watching videos on your player when you're out and about? Deciding this in advance, before you go shopping, can help you narrow the choices – and the chances of confusion – enormously,

If you own an Apple Macintosh computer, it's an even easier decision – get an iPod. These players are designed to work seamlessly with Apple computers so you'll have no problem with incompatibility or differences in file format.

But if you've got a PC and you're buying music online, the choice is less clear-cut. The main problem is that the iPod only works directly with one online music store – Apple's iTunes Music Store. And furthermore the files you buy from there will only play on one portable player – the iPod.

Also, the majority of files you buy from other online stores may not work on the iPod unless they are non-copy-protected MP3 files – and only a few stores sell those. So the bottom line is, if you've got an iPod, you have to use the iTunes player.

This is not a big problem; both the iPod and iTunes are great music players. But, if you've got a PC, and you plan to try out several online music stores, or you have budget considerations, a more flexible non iPod player may be worth investigating.

try this

Many music players will also double as portable hard drives. Use them to carry files, documents, and even programs from place to place (if the storage is big enough).

How much space do I need?

Storage is the most important consideration for a digital music player. The more storage capacity a player has, the more songs, photos and videos it can store – and, of course, the more expensive it is.

For most portable music players storage is measured in gigabytes (Gb) – one gigabyte (1 Gb) is the equivalent of about 240 songs. We strongly recommend that the smallest storage you opt for is 1 Gb – anything less you will quickly find limiting.

At the other end of the scale, the 60 Gb you get with the top-of-the-range iPod is a huge amount of storage – enough for 20,000 songs. Even the most ardent music fan would be hard-pressed to fill it.

You may find the chart below handy for reference.

capacity	songs or	photos or	hours of videos*
1 Gb	240	425	2.5
2 Gb	500	950	5
4 Gb	1,000	1,700	10
5 Gb	1,250	2,125	12.5
10 Gb	2,500	4,250	25
20 Gb	5,000	8,500	50
30 Gb	10,000	12,500	75
60 Gb	20,000	25,000	150

The major players

The several flavours of iPod still dominate the portable music player market. Several other players from respected manufacturers, however, are catching up.

iPod

Still the Rolls Royce in the market and one that's 100 per cent compatible with both Macs and PCs. iPods come in two sizes – 30 and 60 Gb – and two colours, white and black. All models now support photo display and video playback on a high-quality 2.5-in colour display. The iPods boast 20 hours of battery life playing audio, but that drops to 2 hours when watching video.
www.apple.com/ipod
Capacity: 30 Gb/60 Gb – Average price: £220–£300

iPod nano

This elegant, pencil-thin player comes in three capacities – 1, 2 and 4 Gb – and in one of the two signature iPod colours, black or white. The iPod nano's small colour display sports the same menu system as the larger iPods and shows both album art and photos you've uploaded – but it won't play video. Its 14-hour battery life and small size make it particularly good for joggers and gym goers.
www.apple.com/ipodnano/
Capacity: 1 Gb/2 Gb/4 Gb – Average price: £110–£170

iPod shuffle

Despite its lack of screen and relatively small storage of either 0.5 Gb or 1 Gb, the Shuffle's compact design and cheap price have made it a popular accessory even for those who already own an iPod. Songs can only be shuffled or played in strict order – there's no choosing of playlist and other flexibility. The same

weight as a car key, and plugging directly into a computer to charge, the Shuffle, as do most players, doubles up as a mini hard-drive for carrying files around.
www.apple.com/ipodshuffle
Capacity: 0.5 Gb/1 Gb – Average price: £50–£70

Creative Zen Vision: M

Intended to rival Apple's flagship iPods, the Zen does a very good job. It comes in five colours and sports a bright, very high-quality screen, easy to use interface, and excellent battery life. It has a 30-Gb storage capacity, the 'M' supports photo and video playback. But it's also crammed with other features including an FM radio, voice recorders and full compatibility with a host of online outlets. Although the 'M' is slightly bigger and heavier than an iPod, it will still comfortably fit inside most pockets.
www.creative.com/products/mp3/zenvisionm/
Capacity: 30 Gb – Average price: £180

Sony Walkman NW-A100

Sony, of course, invented the Walkman back in the 1980s, and this is their latest version for the digital music age. It's sleek and stylish and very light (just over 100 gms). The interface on the monochrome screen is simple and as easy to use as a mobile phone. Storing 6 Gb of music, the Walkman boasts very good sound quality bolstered by a built-in graphic equalizer and has 14 hours battery life.
Capacity: 6 Gb – Average price: £120–£180

Creative Zen MicroPhoto

Packed with features, this is the main rival to the iPod Nano, but handling double the number of songs on its 8-Gb storage. Like the Zen Vision: M, it sports an FM radio, voice recorder, and photo viewing (photo model only) plus a personal organizer that will sync with your email program. Available in ten different

colours, the MicroPhoto is fully compatible with Windows Media Player and subscription services such as Napster To Go. Its replaceable battery sustains 12 hours of continuous playback.
www.creative.com/products/mp3/zenmicro/
Capacity: 8 Gb – Average price: £180

The best of the rest

Bubbling under the main players is a wide selection of solid and affordable players from a host of manufacturers, both major and minor.

Philips GoGear HDD

Good design and an excellent touch-sensitive interface mark out this player from electronics giant Philips. Like its rivals, the GoGear also features a colour screen, radio tuner and voice recorder. It is also compatible with all good PC-based music services. The battery is non-replaceable, however, and the performance a little slow.
Capacity: 6 Gb–30 Gb – Average price: £120–£180

iRiver H10

This good-value player features a high-end compact design, great sound quality, helped by a graphic equalizer, and an FM radio. The small colour screen supports photo playback. However, the non-intuitive controls and strange interface take a bit of getting used to.
Capacity: 20 Gb – Average price: £120

Toshiba Gigabeat S

Coming in both 30 Gb and 60 Gb capacities, this is the only player that rivals the iPod in terms of storage. Its slick compact design features a 2.4-inch, high-quality screen for viewing photos and video playback. Audio-wise, the Gigabeat plays a number of formats including WMA files and MP3 files. The battery life is particularly good with 12 hours audio playback, dropping to 4 hours for video.
Capacity: 30 Gb/60 Gb – Average price: £160–£200

Setting up your player

Your brand new player's out of the box and ready to go. You've got several music tracks already downloaded and you want to listen to them – now! What next?

must know

We're using the iPod as an example here but the basic browsing, scrolling and playlist functions are common across all other players.

Connecting a player to a computer

Most players connect to sockets on a computer known as USB slots via USB cables. The slots (or ports as they're also called) are found either on the front or at the rear of a PC, while many laptops and some Macs may have them to the side. When connected to both a player and a computer, the USB cable will allow you to transfer music (and other files) to-and-fro between the player and the computer at a speed of around one song a second. The cable will also charge your player – although this may take longer than just plugging it into the wall with the separate power adaptor.

Make sure your player is on and then plug it into your USB slot. Expect a short delay as your computer works to recognize your device.

If you are using a PC, you will receive a notification (similar to the one shown left) at the bottom of your computer screen.

Shortly after, as long as everything is okay, your player will appear as a 'Removable Device' under 'My Computer'.

On the Mac, any connected players appear in the left-hand side of the Finder window. Just click on the hard disk icon on your desktop to reveal this window.

Filling up your player

Once you've connected your player, it's time to start loading the music. Many players at this point will fill up automatically – a process known as synchronization (see page 122). New files and purchased songs will be copied over without you having to lift a finger.

If you've chosen to manually update your player, you can opt to copy an entire playlist. To learn how to set up playlists see page 93.

Disconnecting your player

First, before you pull the wire out, click on the arrow icon next to the iPod name to disconnect. Wait until the iPod icon disappears from the desktop. This should take less than 10 seconds, but it can take as long as a minute if your computer is busy. As your iPod is no longer showing on the main menu, then it is now safe to disconnect it.

On a PC there is an additional step of removing hardware. Right-click the green arrow icon in the taskbar at the bottom of the screen, and choose 'Remove hardware'. On the next screen, select the iPod and click on 'Stop'. After a moment your PC will tell you it is safe to remove your player.

As soon as your iPod is connected to your computer, the battery will start charging. You can tell how much power your iPod has by examining the green battery icon in the top right corner. If it is switched to red in colour, that means it is very low on juice. It usually takes an hour to charge an iPod to full capacity. Some players take up to two hours to charge.

watch out!

Don't disconnect a player from the computer unless it tells you that it is safe to do so. Data can still be dribbling between the two machines and you could lose some if you yank the cable prematurely.

iPod: Battery icon - charging

Using a player

Just like the portable CDs and minidisk players that preceded them, today's digital music players are designed to be simple for anyone to use.

The basics

Connecting the headphones

Just slip the supplied headphones into the socket on your player. On the larger iPods and the Zen Micro you'll find the socket at the top. On the iPod nano, the socket is on the bottom. You can use any pair of headphones with your player.

Playing a song

Slide your finger gently in a clockwise direction around the central grey wheel of the iPod, known as the Click Wheel. This will move the blue highlight bar down (or up if you move your finger anti-clockwise). Stop on 'Music' and click the centre button. The Music menu will appear. Choose 'Songs' from this menu and hit 'Select' again. A list of your songs will appear; click on one to play it.

Changing the volume

To alter the volume while a song is playing, gently turn the Click Wheel – clockwise will boost the volume, anti-clockwise will reduce it. A blue bar – and the sound in your headphones, of course – will give you an indication of how loud the player is.

Pausing and skipping

To pause a song, hit the 'Play/Pause' area on the lower part of the Click Wheel. A Pause icon will appear in the top left-hand corner. To skip a track, tap the right-hand area of the Click Wheel once. Click the left-hand area to go back a track.

Fast forward and rewind

If you want to skip past a part of song you don't like, press and hold the fast-forward button. You'll hear your music judder and skip like a jumping CD. Don't worry – that's what digital music sounds like when it's fast-forwarding. To fast rewind, press and hold the rewind button. Let go of the button to resume playing.

The 'Hold' button

The 'Hold' button is one of the most important buttons on your iPod. Flip it – push it to the right until the orange strip is visible – and all the controls are frozen. This stops you accidentally brushing the 'Stop' button or the Click Wheel while the player's knocking around in your pocket or bag.

Maximizing battery life

The battery life on an iPod is around 14 hours. But if you use the screen a lot, this will diminish massively. If you want to stretch the battery life, use the screen as little as possible. Better still set the Backlight Timer to as short a period as possible. To do this, choose 'Settings' from the main menu and then Backlight Timer. Opt for two seconds, and you'll extend your battery life.

Checking space

At some point you may need to check if you've got enough storage space on your iPod for any additional tracks you've downloaded onto your computer. To do this choose 'Settings' and then 'About' from the iPod menu. A screen will appear detailing the number of songs already on your iPod and the amount of space left available. As a rough guide 100 Mb is about 24 songs, while 1 Gb is 240.

> **want to know more?**
> • To save space on screen switch iTunes to 'minimode'. On a PC, under the 'Advanced' menu, choose 'Switch To Mini Player'. On a Mac, click on the green plus (+) sign in the top left of the iTunes window to toggle between mini and full modes.
>
> **weblinks**
> • For information on all things iPod and out-and-out pod worship try: www.ilounge.com
> • Get the latest updates for Windows Media Player at: www.micro soft.com/windows/ windowsmedia/
> • For plugins, add-ons and updates for iTunes: www.apple.com/itunes

4 Buying music online

Your portable player is full. You've burnt several CDs. You're probably eager now to join the internet digital music revolution and start buying and downloading songs. In this chapter, we're going to take you on a tour of the best online shops for music and show you how to navigate the various offers, technologies and software you need to get started. We'll also give you tips on controlling your spending, because once you see how quick and easy downloading music is, you'll be hooked. That's guaranteed.

Online music stores

Whether online music outlets will ever replace the high-street record store remains to be seen, but without doubt they are a quick, cheap and excellent way to discover and buy music.

must know

To simplify the tangle of different file formats and copy-protection schemes, Microsoft have created a single standard, or kite mark, known as Plays For Sure. If your player and the music site you're using both display the Plays For Sure logo, downloaded tracks will play without any problems. Visit www.playsforsure.com

Paying for downloads

Online music stores come in two main flavours – pay-per-download and subscription 'rental' sites.

With pay-per-download stores, such as iTunes, once you've paid and downloaded your track, you can burn it to CD, copy it to your iPod and transfer it to any other computer. There are a few restrictions (see below) but this is the model a lot of sites copy.

Subscription outlets are 'all you can eat'. You pay a monthly fee and are allowed to stream, but not download, as many tracks as you like, essentially using the site as an online jukebox. If you want to own a specific track, you can pay a download fee.

Some subscription sites, such as Rhapsody, also allow you to download a certain amount of tracks and store them on your portable player only – not your computer. This is to stop you making copies.

Many of these shops offer free trial periods, so it's worth trying several until you find one you like.

DRM (Digital Rights Management)

DRM is an important concept to understand as you browse the digital music world – it basically means copy-protection. Essentially, if you download a song with DRM, there are certain limits as to what you can do with the track. This depends on the type of DRM but usually it's some form of copy-protection.

Apple's Fairplay DRM, for example, means you can copy each track to five other computers and burn it as many times as you want onto CD. But the tracks only work on one portable player – Apple's iPod.

DRM-free tracks, however, are yours to do with whatever you want. Once you've paid for the download, you can burn it onto CD, transfer it onto your portable player, or copy it onto a computer.

Which store?
Apple's iTunes Music Store continues to expand and dominate the online music world, but others are up and coming.

iTunes Music Store (PC/Mac)
The first and still the best, Apple's iTunes Music Store started the revolution and continues to be the market leader. Its great-looking interface has the biggest selection of high profile and independent artists online – along with podcasts, weekly free tracks, and TV programmes (in some regions). But at £0.99p ($0.99c) a track it's one of the most expensive. Downloaded tracks will only play in the iTunes player and on the iPod.
www.apple.com/itunes/music/

Napster (PC only)
The reborn Napster has two types of service. One is the streaming service, in which you can stream the entire catalogue on your computer – all two million songs – for the monthly fee of £9.95, but you cannot download anything. If you like a song, however, you can pay £0.79p ($0.99c) to download it.
www.napster.com

PC: IE: Napster homepage.

PC: IE: Napster To Go homepage.

PC: IE: Rhapsody homepage.

PC: IE: eMusic homepage.

Napster To Go (PC only)

For £14.95 a month this innovative service allows you to download over 80 hours of music onto specific, accredited players such as the Creative Zen range, Dell's Pocket DJ, and iRiver's H10. The tracks are protected ensuring that you cannot play them on your computer or any other players, nor can you burn them to CD. But if you mostly listen to music on the move, this is a great deal. www.napster.com

Rhapsody (PC/Mac)

This US service has one of the largest selections of music and its downloads are compatible with all players, including iPods. The high-quality tracks cost $0.79c per track or $14.95 monthly 'rental' for unlimited downloads (NB the rental service doesn't work on iPods). www.real/.com/rhapsody

eMusic (PC/Mac)

This site focuses on independent labels and up-and-coming artists, so can be a bit low on big names. All the MP3 songs are DRM-free, meaning you can play them on any computer and any player. The price is $9.99 to download 40 tracks – $0.25 a track – the cheapest online. www.emusic.com/

Windows Media Player selection (PC only)

Not technically one store, but over ten merged together as a single 'integrated' store, accessible by clicking on the 'Buy Music' button in Windows Media Player. There's a very wide range of music available. The high-quality downloads can be played on up to five different computers and copied to the bulk of players on the market. http://music.msn.com/

The best of the rest

Everyone's climbing aboard the digital music bandwagon – shops, retailers and even mobile phone companies. Here are some worth exploring.

Sony Connect (PC only)

Only compatible with Sony portable players such as the new Walkman and the PlayStation Portable (see page 184–5). www.connect.com

MusicMatch (PC only)

Good selection of over 800,00 tracks for $9.95 a month or $0.99c a track. www.musicmatch.com/download/

Bleep (PC/Mac)

Left-field and electronic music for £0.99 a track, or £6.99 an album. Free previews and download high-quality DRM free MP3 files. www.bleep.com/

HMV Digital (PC only)

For just £14.99 a month HMV Digital provides access to 1.8 million songs, including exclusive tracks. Read the small print though; downloaded tracks are subject to many restrictions. www.hmv.co.uk/hmvweb/

PlayLouder

Cool tracks for a younger audience. Up to three free tracks a month. www.playlouder.com/downloads/

Virgin

All-you-can-stream service for £7.99–£14.99 a month. www.virgindigital.com

Shopping tips

With so much music on offer online, finding exactly what you want can sometimes be frustrating. Here are some tips to help you maximize your online shopping experience at the iTunes Music Store.

Free songs

Every week, iTunes has a free track to download, usually by a fairly well-known artist. The link is usually in the centre of the iTunes Music Store homepage, although it does move around. Click on it and you'll be transported to a mini-homepage where you can preview and then download all the available tracks.

iTunes free single of the week page.

Genre Browsing

Click on the eye in the top right-hand corner. This activates Genre Browsing, a much easier way of looking for music. The screen breaks into columns. The first column lists the broad category – comedy, blues, rock, indie etc. Click on one of these and a set of subgenres will appear, for example, Hard Rock, Blues and Psychedelic all appear under Rock. Next a list of artists linked to each subgenre will appear. You can then narrow it still further as individual albums appear in the next column.

All this time, the lower window will be filling up with tracks. This will gradually get shorter as you filter your tracks through more and more columns. This method of browsing is a great way of finding specific tracks – especially obscure ones. You might also be exposed to music you've never heard of, in a genre or subgenre of music you particularly like.

Skim Previews

Often there will be several versions of the song you want but it's not always clear from the title that the track you're about to preview is the correct one. Don't worry, however, as there's no need to listen to the entire preview. If it's not the right track just click the right-arrow key on your keyboard to immediately skip to the next version.

Find an artist's entire work

If you want to see all the material an artist has available, click on the small grey circle with the arrow after the artist's name. This takes you to the artist's own homepage and a full catalogue on iTunes. Some artists also have extra details, such as biographies and pictures.

Emailing a song link

Sending a friend a link to the song is easy. Just open a new email and then click-and-drag either the song's album cover or the song's title into the main message area of the email window. A direct link to the song on iTunes will appear like a normal weblink.

Checking you don't already have a song

If you have a big music collection, accidentally buying a song you already own can become a common danger. To check whether or not you already own a song, hold down the Ctrl key (Mac: Apple key) and click on the grey arrow to the right of the artist's name in the track list window. This flips you back to the music library on your computer and lists all the tracks you already have by that particular artist. A quick scan of the list should show you whether you're about to waste your money.

See the album art

One thing old-fashioned CD music has over digital music is the cover art. A beautiful sleeve can increase your appreciation of a song or album. The sleeves are still there in iTunes; in fact many are quite big, especially if you buy them direct from the store. First, activate song artwork with the 'Show Artwork' option under the 'Edit' menu. Then click directly on the album image to display a larger, perhaps even super-huge version of the album cover.

Celebrity Playlists

If you're stuck for musical inspiration or just fancy hearing something new, go to the iTunes homepage and click on Celebrity Playlists (left side of the window; you may have to scroll down). There you will find the top ten playlist of famous musicians and celebrities. Just click on a person's face to see his or her selections. 'See All' will reveal the vast list of people who have already submitted their playlists.

Blocking explicit lyrics

Some tracks on iTunes are labelled explicit. You may not want certain members of your family, children especially, accessing or hearing these tracks – with iTunes they can be blocked easily.

Under File menu (Mac: iTunes menu), select the 'Preferences' option and then click on the 'Parental' icon. You'll see an option to restrict explicit content. Click the tickbox next to it. If you want to make sure this option is not bypassed, click on the 'Padlock' in the corner; now only someone with your password can change or revert the settings.

Sending a song as a gift

In fact you can send an entire album, or even a music video, to a friend as a present. Find the artist's page for the song you like, and click the 'Gift This Music' link. This takes you to a special page where you can choose individual songs from that artist. Follow the instructions and within minutes your friend will be emailed a link where they can download the song.

Searching tips

Relevance

Search results are usually arranged in order of relevance – in other words, how closely they match the song name, artist, or any other details you searched for. This is depicted as a bar in the relevant column. The longer the bar, the more accurate the hit.

Re-sort

It's a good idea to re-sort your results as the number of returns you get can number in the thousands. Click on the word 'Artist' for example to alphabetically order the results by artist. Clicking the top bar repeatedly toggles between downwardly ordered lists and upwardly ordered lists.

Powersearch

If you still have not found what you want, or you need a particularly obscure track, click on the 'Powersearch' button on the left-hand side of the iTunes Music Store homepage. A more detailed search box will appear, allowing you to search in multiple areas such as composer, genre, year, etc. It gives you a chance to streamline and add more detail to your search.

Controlling your spending

Shopping for music online is so easy and so quick, that it's all too easy for purchases to get out of hand. Before you know it you can easily rack up hundreds of downloads and be horrified when you receive the bill.

Activating a shopping cart.

Checking your account.

Setting up an allowance.

Use a shopping cart

The Shopping Cart on iTunes Music Store is disabled by default, so go to 'Preferences' and under the green 'Store' icon, you'll find an option to 'Buy using a Shopping Cart'. Now when you purchase songs online they will end up in your Shopping Cart, giving you a chance to review – and take a deep breath – before committing to buying and downloading them.

Track your spending

There's a useful feature built into the iTunes Music Store that allows you to see how much you've spent, when, and on what. Click on the 'Account' button in the upper right-hand corner of the iTunes studio. Enter your password and then press the 'View Account' button to see all your info. Click on 'Purchase History' and you'll see a nicely laid out invoice with all your purchases listed. This should give you a sense of perspective.

Set up an allowance

A good way to control your spending and those of anyone else who might be using your computer is a download allowance. Once set up, each month a certain amount will be credited to the account and debited from your credit card. To activate it, scan the left-hand list of links on the homepage and select 'Monthly Gift', and fill in the form, entering the amount you want to gift each month. Apple will also send a note to you or anyone else who shares your account informing them of the allowance.

Block unauthorized people

If you sell your computer, the person who buys it may well be able to access your iTunes account, even if you wipe the hard disk. This is because the authorization process uses a snapshot of your computer's hardware, which doesn't change, even if you erase your files. The best way to avoid this is to 'deauthorize' your computer before you sell it. Under the 'Advanced' menu in iTunes, select 'Deauthorize Computer'. Warning: only do this if you really are selling or passing your machine to someone else.

Deauthorizing your computer.

want to know more?

• If you've got a slow connection, you can speed up your previews. Under the iTunes menu, click 'Preferences' and then the 'Store' icon. Tick the option that reads 'Load Complete Preview' before playing.
• If you're annoyed with your downloaded tracks having copyright protection (DRM), there's an easy way to bypass it. Just burn the tracks onto an audio CD. Then, insert the CD back into your computer and rip the tracks to your computer (page 86). Now your copies have no DRM.

weblinks
• For a list of current online music stores go to: www.http://en.wiki pedia.org/wiki/Online_ music_store
• For a review of online stores: www.extreme tech.com/article2/0,169 7,1784353,00.asp

5 Digital music collections

You're now armed with all the gadgets and
tools you need to start building a full digital
music collection. This is where the real power
of downloadable music starts to shine. In this
chapter we'll show you how to convert your
own music CDs into digital music files easily
and simply without falling foul of the various
file formats. We'll also explain how to use the
advanced features of iTunes and Windows
Media Player (WMP) to keep your burgeoning
collection organized and easy to search. Finally,
we'll introduce you to playlists – a powerful way
to create new and unexpected collections of
your songs.

Digitizing music CDs

The first step in building your digital music collection will most likely be digitizing, or 'ripping', your existing CD collection into a digital music player program such as Windows Media Player or iTunes. It's easy to do and won't harm your CDs.

must know

On websites and in some programs, digitizing is often referred to as 'ripping'. Don't worry - this is just Internet slang and no physical damage is actually done to either the compact disc or the computer.

Today's music scene

The bulk of your music collection is probably on CD. That's no good, really, for today's computer-centred, download-driven music scene. If you want to listen to them on your computer or a portable player, you need to digitize them.

Digitizing is simple. It involves inserting the audio CD into your computer, copying the contents over, track by track, and encoding them into a compressed digital music file format, such as MP3.

With today's fast computers, digitizing an entire CD usually takes under ten minutes, but if you use a really fast computer, it can take as little as two minutes. Once the tracks have been digitized onto your computer, they then exist as files, just like documents or photos. That means they can be ordered, stacked in your music player, loaded onto your iPod, emailed to other people, or proudly exhibited in your digital music collection. You can even make copies and back them up.

File formats

As ever, there is a vast array of confusingly different file formats to consider before you start ripping your music. The standard digital file format is the MP3 file. All formats are essentially very similar but with

just minor technical and sound quality differences.
We go through them in more detail on pages 27-9
but you can use this quick chart as a reference.

File	Description	Restrictions	Quality
MP3	Universal format	Works in all players	Good
WMA	Microsoft format	PC mostly; won't play in iTunes	Excellent
AAC / M4A / M4B	Apple format	Purchased files will only play on Macs and iPods	Excellent
WAV	Microsoft uncompressed format	None	Top
AIFF	Apple's uncompressed format	None	Top
OGG	Independent format	Need special software plugins to play	Excellent

File	Play on iPod?	Play on other players	Copy protection (DRM)
MP3	Yes	All	None
WMA	No	Yes	Yes
AAC / M4A / M4B	Yes	A few	Yes sometimes
WAV	Yes	Some	No
AIFF	Yes	No	No
OGG	No	A few	No

must know

Apple's digital music format – the AAC file
– has four different versions. They are:
TRACK4.AAC – normal AAC file, no copy
protection
TRACK4.M4A – also a normal AAC file with
no copy protection
TRACK4.M4P – AAC file with protection
TRACK4.M4B – iTunes Music Store Spoken
Word file, like an audiobook.

How to digitize a CD

Step 1

Insert the CD and wait a few moments for the computer to read and check the CD.

To see what's on the CD, in Windows Media Player, click on the 'Rip' tab.

Step 2

In iTunes, click on the name of the CD in the left-hand window. A list of the contents of the CD will appear as Track 1, Track 2, but without track names.

If your computer cannot read the track names from the CD there are two things you can do. If you are connected to the Internet, you can use an online track name database to download the track names. If you're not online, you'll have to enter the track names manually. Skip to step 4.

Step 3

To get the track names, your computer must connect to an online database. The process is free and more or less instant. In WMP, click on the 'Find Album Info' in the top left corner.

Step 4

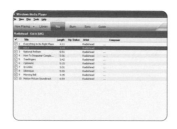

On the preferences screen, select the 'Advanced' tab.

In iTunes, under the 'Advanced' menu, choose 'Get CD Track Names '. Doing this should fill not just the track and artist name, but the album name and any other details that are in the database.

Sometimes, rarely, getting the CD tracks names from the Internet doesn't work. This may be either because the online database is busy (in that case try again in a few minutes). Otherwise, the CD you've inserted may be unknown on the database. That's either because it's very obscure, rare or it's a home-made CD. Compilation CDs made for you by friends on recordable CDs for example won't be recognized.

Step 5

Before you start digitizing your music collection, you should decide what file format you're going to use. Check the table on page 28 to see the advantages and disadvantages of each. The main issue is whether you're going to convert all your music into MP3 format, which is the general format, or whether you're going to opt for AAC, which is a Mac-only or mostly Mac format. If you own a Mac and an iPod, you're best digitizing your music as AAC, which provides slightly better audio quality than MP3. However, if you intend to share your music on a PC, or have a different portable music player, you may want to choose the MP3 format for all your music.

In WMP, under the 'Tools' menu, select 'Options' and then the 'Rip Music' tag. Under 'Rip Settings', you can decide the file format you want to use.

In iTunes, choose 'Preferences' under the iTunes menu. Click on the 'Advanced' icon and then select the 'Importing' tag. You'll find a pull-down menu where you can chose your file format.

Ripping preferences in WMP.

Ripping preferences in iTunes.

Step 6

On the same screen, you can also decide what quality of digital music you want. Most players are set, by default, to digitize at the average quality of digital music. It can get a bit technical, but generally speaking quality for digital music is rated in kilobits per second (kb/s). That's how many slices of data (kilobits) represent the music per second – the higher the better. The average bit rate for digital music is 128 kb/s, but some people say a rate of 192 kb/s sounds better. At 256 kb/s, most people agree the quality is indistinguishable from CD audio.

But remember, the higher the quality, the bigger the resulting file. So a 3-minute song at 128 kb/s will be around 3 Mb. At 256 kb/s, it'll be closer to 6 Mb. So, if you're short of space on your hard disk or portable player – and you don't have the fussy ears of a hi-fi shop manager – you can just stick with 128 kb/s and fit twice as many songs on your player.

Step 7

Now you're ready to rip. In WMP, just select the 'Grab' button and the process will unfold automatically. In iTunes, hit the round 'Import CD' icon in the top left corner. Depending on the speed of your CD drive, each track can take between 30 seconds and 5 minutes to rip.

Step 8

If you were unable to identify your track names earlier, you'll have to type them manually once they've been copied to your computer. Just click in the field for each category (artist, song, etc.) and copy the details from your CD's sleeve. Try to make sure you get the spelling correct as this will help you find and sort tracks more accurately in your collection later.

Congratulations – you've just grabbed your first CD.

must know

Windows Media Player may ask if you want to add copy-protection on the file you grab. Select 'No'. You want to share them easily, right?

Organizing your collection

As you start to download music, rip music CDs, and share music, your collection will grow rapidly. Hundreds of songs from myriad artists will fill up your hard disk. So it's very important to have a system early on and to learn how to organize your collection before your musical garden turns into a cacophonous jungle.

Tagging

You can keep tags on your growing music collection by literally keeping tags. Each digital music file has what's know as an ID3 tag which stores important information about that file – the artist, the song title, the year and so on. Think of it as a digital label.

Most of this data is optional, but it's important that you keep your ID3 tags current and correct, so that both you and your computer can recognize the file and organize it correctly. This data will also come in handy when you come to making Auto Playlists (see page 93).

Editing your tags

If you spot errors or gaps in your tags, there are two ways to edit them:

Windows Media Player (PC)

In the Library window, right-click on a track. On the menu that appears choose 'Edit'. You'll be able to type whatever you like into the field.

To go a bit deeper in the track's tags, choose 'Advanced Tag Editor' from the same menu. There you can alter title, genre, mood – even the musical key the track was recorded in, if you know it.

iTunes (PC/Mac)

In the Library window, click inside the field you want to change, such as artist, year, etc., and then type the information that needs to go there.

Alternatively you can select a file and press CTRL + I (Mac: Apple + I). This brings up the additional information window. Click on the 'Info' tab at the top to see a list of fields you can edit.

How to really trash the place

If you're deleting a track in a playlist, hitting the 'Delete' key will only remove it from the playlist, not from your library. If you really want it gone from your life, you need to be on the Library screen before you can fully delete it. In Windows Media Player, this means having 'All Music' highlighted in the left-hand window. In iTunes, select 'Library'.

Ratings

As you listen and relisten to your library of songs, you'll start to like some tracks more than others. Sometimes, like early on a Monday morning, you'll only want to listen to your most uplifting tracks. If you get in the habit of rating songs from one star to five, you can use these scores to easily organize the best of your tracks.

To rate a song, just click in the rating column. Then click on the top of the 'Ratings' column to sort your songs so that the highest-rated tracks appear at the top.

In Windows Media Player, click on the 'Burn' tab and on the resulting screen choose 'Purchased Music' from the 'Burn List' menu. Finally, follow the onscreen commands.

must know

If you have a change of heart, don't worry. A deleted file is only moved to the Recycle Bin (or Trash Can on the Apple Mac). As long as you haven't emptied the bin, you can fish it out from there if you want to keep it.

In iTunes, select the 'Purchased Songs' playlist in the left-hand window and then hit the 'Burn Disc' icon in the top right of the screen. Now your purchased music will be backed up and you can breathe easily.

Burning data CDs

If you have a lot of tracks to back up, it may be best to burn a 'data disc' rather than an audio disc. This way you can store far more tracks on each CD or DVD – around 100 on a CD, or up to a 1,000 on a DVD. Although you cannot back up purchased files in this manner, you can certainly make copies of tracks you've digitized, so it's a great way of backing up your music collection.

iTunes (PC/Mac)

Under the File menu (Mac: iTunes menu), select 'Preferences' and then the 'Advanced' tab. Choose 'Burning' and you'll see options asking you what type of disc you'd like to burn. Select 'Data CD'.

Windows Media Player (PC only)

When on the 'Burn' screen, pull down the menu above the CD window and various options will appear. Choose 'Data CD' from the list. That's it.

must know

The main danger with having a digital music collection is that you could lose it if your computer hard disk fails. If you've purchased and downloaded music it may mean you'll have to buy your music all over again. The best way to back-up your music collection is onto a portable music player. Another quick and easy way is to burn your most precious songs – or the ones you've bought at least – to CD or DVD.

Playlists

At the core of your music collection is the playlist – a list of songs gathered into one file. It could feature all the tracks from your favourite album, or all 300 songs recorded by your favourite artists.

Using playlists

Playlists are the best and most powerful way to organize digital music. A playlist can contain any number of tracks so you can create a compilation for a party or the running order of a CD. You can make a playlist yourself or have your digital music player generate one for you, based on your mood, your ratings, or just randomly. Playlists are also the best way of copying tracks to and from a portable player. You can also share them online.

Exploring playlists

Both Windows Media Player (WMP) and iTunes have a selection of simple playlists built-in. In the left-hand window of WMP's 'Library' screen, for example, you'll see an option called 'Auto Playlists'. Click on the '+' next to it and a handful of playlists will scroll down. These include 'Fresh Tracks', 'Music tracks I have not rated', and so on.

Similarly, in iTunes, in the left-hand window, you'll see playlists such as 'Five star rated' and 'Party Shuffle'. These are all 'Auto' or 'Smart' playlists which are explored on page 97. Right now we're going to concentrate on creating simple playlists.

Creating a playlist in Windows Media Player (PC only)

1 With the 'Library' tab selected at the top of the screen, right-click on the 'My Playlist' option in the left-hand window and select 'New...' from the menu.

2 A blue window will appear on the right. Text inside invites you to 'Drag items here to build a list of items for your playlist.'

3 Now, in the left-hand window, select 'All Music' to bring up your full library list of tracks. Select some tracks you like and drag them into the 'New Playlist' window.

4 When you've finished making your selection, right-click anywhere inside the 'New Playlist' window and choose 'Save Playlist...' from the menu that appears.

5 Digital music collections

5 Type a name and hit the 'Save' button. Your playlist is now added to your library.

6 Your newly created playlist appears in the right-hand window. If you want to add more tracks, just drag them over onto the 'Playlist' icon.

Creating a playlist in iTunes (PC/Mac)

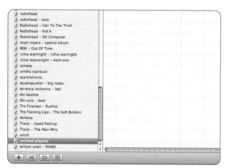

1 Click on the plus (+) icon in the bottom left-hand corner. A new 'untitled' playlist icon will appear along the left-hand side of the screen, represented by a blue icon with a black musical note inside.

2 Type in the name you want for your playlist, or leave it blank until you're ready to name it.

watch out!

If you delete a track from a playlist it is not removed from your computer, only from that playlist. The track in a playlist only refers to the original, which still exists in your library until it is deleted.

3 If you click on the playlist, the contents will be displayed in the main library window. If your playlist is empty, the screen will be blank.

4 To get your full library back just click on the yellow library icon at the top of the screen.

5 To fill up a playlist, just select a track or tracks from the library and drag them onto your playlist icon.

6 The tracks will now be inside the playlist and will play in the order that they appear.

try this

Another way to make a playlist is to select a chunk of tracks from your library and then choose 'New Playlist' from the File menu. All the tracks are now gathered into a single neat playlist.

Removing songs from a playlist

Deleting songs from your playlist is done in the same way as deleting other items. Just highlight the track and press the 'Delete' key.

Ordering songs in playlists

By default, tracks on your playlists are placed in the order you added them to the list. Depending on how you want them arranged, you can re-order them any way you like.

In Windows Media Player, right-click on a track name and then select 'Move Up' or 'Move Down' from the menu. In iTunes, just click and drag the song to where you want it to be in the playing order.

Deleting playlists

If you want to delete a playlist, click on it with the right mouse button on the PC (Mac: Ctrl + click) and a mini-menu will appear. Choose the 'Delete' option and the playlist will be sent to the trash. Note: only the playlist goes – your songs remain in your main library.

How long is my playlist?

It's useful sometimes to know just how long a playlist is or how long it'll take you to listen to the entire thing, especially if you're running short of space on your iPod. Look at the bottom of the screen and you'll see a running total of the playlists' sizes: in minutes and megabytes. The megabytes field is particularly useful. If you're burning a playlist to CD (pages 57-9), you'll need to make sure the total doesn't exceed 650Mbs, which is the maximum capacity of a standard CD.

watch out!

If you're using iTunes, make sure 'Shuffle' is off at the bottom of the screen. If it's on, you will not be able to change the order.

Auto and Smart playlists

With Auto and Smart playlists, the true power of digital music starts to come into play. Most of the functionality we've been dealing with until now can be emulated on a hi-fi or portable music player. But Auto or Smart playlists allow you to become truly digitally creative.

Be smart

Smart playlists are not only a good way in which to organize your music collection, but they also throw in surprises when you're listening to your music. Furthermore, Smart playlists push up old, obscure tracks from the depths of your collection and keep your music listening vital and exciting.

What is a Smart playlist?

A Smart playlist (or smartlist) uses the tags attached to songs to build and auto-generate playlists. So, for example, you can create a playlist of your least played or your most played track. All this can be done with just a few mouse clicks.

In addition, smartlists are updated live. This means that any changes to your library such as adding new tracks, deleting songs, changing star ratings – are mirrored instantly in your smartlists.

In Windows Media Player, these kinds of smartlists are called Auto playlists and are denoted by a green icon with a circular green arrow. In iTunes, they're called Smart playlists and are represented by purple icons. They're exactly the same feature in both players and work more or less the same. We'll refer to them both as 'smartlists'.

> **try this**
> You can create a smartlist for every occasion and take it with you. For example, make a selection of fast songs called 'Running' or dance tunes called 'Parties', then copy them onto your portable music player.

Create a smartlist in iTunes

1 Under the FIle menu, you need to select 'New Smart Playlist ...'.

2 The first field is the criteria by which you're going to choose your tracks. This can be almost anything – genre, rating, artists, size, time, etc.

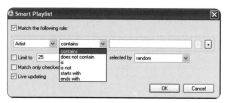

3 The next field allows you to refine the first criterion, for example by including only those tracks with the words 'sugar' or 'rock' in the title.

4 If you want to add further criteria, click on the big plus (+) sign at the end of the line. The big minus (–) sign on the other hand removes criteria. Add and remove criteria until you've reached the level of refinement you want.

5 The example smartlist shown here will collate all songs by Mozart with a rating of two stars or higher, which will fit onto a single CD. Hit 'OK' and you're done.

Create a smartlist in Windows Media Player

1 With the Library tab activated, right-click on Auto Playlists in the left-hand window and choose 'New Auto Playlist ...'.

2 Give your smartlist a name and then click on the first green plus (+) sign to add the first criterion.

3 Each criterion has an underlined keyword. Click on these to reveal more options to help you refine the criteria even more.

4 Choose an option from the pull-down menu and then keep clicking on the plus (+) sign, adding criteria until you're happy.

5 If you want to limit the size or running time of the playlist to ensure the contents fit on a CD for example, click on the 'add restriction' field and choose an option from the menu.

6 The Auto Playlist shown here will collate all the rock songs you've listened to in the last 30 days that are under 3 minutes in length

Advanced smartlists

Here are some examples of fun smartlists you can create with just a few clicks of the mouse.

Genre smartlist

Got a lot of jazz in your collection? Indie? Rock? Calypso? You can hoop all those tracks in a single, automatically generated list. The smartlist shown here will gather all the jazzy tracks in the collection by examining the genre tags and then pulling in not just 'jazz' but also 'jazz'-related genres such as smooth jazz, easy listening and so on.

Least played smartlist

Both iTunes and Windows Media Player automatically create smartlists containing your most highly rated songs. But what about your least favourite songs? This fun smartlist chucks all your lowest rated songs in a digital heap for you to pick through.

Short attention span smartlist

This exacting smartlist scoops together all tracks under 2 minutes 30 seconds and collects them into a playing order that only lasts 10 minutes. And by selecting random order, every time you select this smartlist, different tracks will appear.

Slow songs only smartlist

Some songs, especially dance tracks, are now tagged with the beats per minutes (BPM), which gives their precise tempo making it easier for DJs to mix the tracks together. Many of your tracks won't have BPMs but some might. Run this smartlist and see which slow dance tunes appear.

My favourite tracks from 1990 smartlist

By combining just the year 1990 and the number of times you've listened and rated tracks, you can build a very selective playlist that collates your stand out tunes for a particular year.

My top 100

Curious to know what your current all-time top 100 would be? This smartlist will generate exactly that, based on your listening habits.

Everything in its right place

Now you know how to rip, there is an essential action you must carry out. A digital music collection works far better if all your music sits in one single folder on your computer. So you need to create a directory where all your music can be stored.

On a Windows-based PC computer, this is most likely to be the 'My Music' directory. You'll find it if you right click the mouse button on the 'My Computer' icon and then choose 'My Documents'.

On an Apple Macintosh computer, open the Finder by double-clicking on the hard drive icon on your desktop. You'll see a list of file locations down the side (Desktop, Movies etc.). Choose 'Music' from this list. That's your music directory.

You can choose your own directory to put your music in, if you like. You may, for example, have two hard disks in your computer and wish to dedicate one to music. That's fine. Whether you use the default one or create a new one, however, it's essential you tell your music player where this directory is. That way it will always know where to put any purchased or ripped music.

want to know more?

• Try setting a music folder in iTunes or in Windows Media Player.
• Make sure the option that reads 'Copy files to iTunes Music Folder when adding to library' is checked. That way all new music files will always end up in that folder.
• CDs were meant to be indestructible but they're not. When digitized, scratches can be converted to static and distortion in the resulting digital files. It is always advisable to wipe any smears, dust or hairs from a CD before ripping.

weblinks
• If you want to be introduced to new music based on your existing music tastes, try these music recommendation sites:
www.last.fm
www.pandora.com/

6 Using player programs

Now you've learned the basics of digital music – such as how to digitize all your music, play it, order it in a variety of ways, and take it with you on the move – it's time to master the digital player. On one level a digital player such as iTunes or Windows Media Player (WMP) is just that, a player, not much more than a hi-fi. But beneath the surface of these powerful programs lie all sorts of hidden features and powerful tools. In this chapter, we'll show you how to get the most out of your player, how to change its look and feel, create new genres to organize your music, and how to make your player the centrepiece of any party.

Advanced player

Allow us to take you beyond the play button and show you some of the many exciting things you can do with your player. You'll be amazed by how much power you have at your fingertips.

Date added

If you're editing your view options, 'Date Added' is a very useful column to opt for. If you sort your library by 'Date Added' (click on the word 'Date Added' at the top of the column), all the freshest tracks in your library will automatically be lined up for you to play.

Editing multiple songs

If you want to change the information on several songs at a time, for example to mark them all as belonging to the same album, or give several songs the same rating simultaneously, you need to use a two-stage process.

iTunes (PC/Mac)

1 Select the tracks you want.

2 Now Ctrl + click (Mac: Apple + click) on your multiple tracks. On the mini menu that will next appear, choose 'Get Info ...'.

must know

Don't worry if you make a mistake, the changes are not permanent. You can repeat the process as many times as you want.

3 A warning box may appear asking: 'Are you sure you want to edit information for multiple items?' Click 'Yes'.

4 Now enter any information you want to in these boxes. When you click 'OK', all the information you've entered will be stamped onto your selected files.

Windows Media Player (PC only)

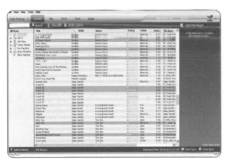

1 Select the tracks you want.

2 Right-click on your multiple tracks and choose 'Advanced Tag Editor'.

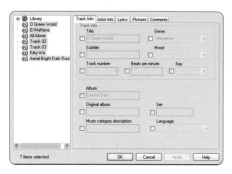

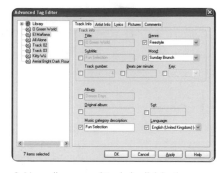

3 In the screen that appears you'll see all your tracks lined up on the left and several fields for the information you can change arranged on the right by category: track info, artists info, lyrics, pictures, and so on.

4 Now all you need to do is click in the text boxes alongside the fields to change the details.

try this

If you want to quickly add a genre when you're browsing your library, click in the Genre column and type in the name of your new genre. It'll be added to the overall genre list.

Creating genres

Genres are very useful for organizing your collection and for exploring different types of music, from classical to conga. Sometimes, however, you may need to create your own genres, especially as iTunes doesn't include more obscure genres such as Death Metal, Salsa and ElectroClash.

To create your own genre in iTunes, right-click (Mac: Ctrl + click) on any song, and then select 'Get Info' from the menu. Click on the 'Info' tab at the top of the next screen and enter the name of your new genre in the labelled panel at the bottom.

In Windows Media Player, just right-click on a track and choose 'Advanced Tag Editor' from the menu.

On some occasions though a song will not fit into a single genre. It could be a rock track with jazzy elements or a dance track with a Bossa Nova feel. If you have tracks like this you can also create a 'meta-genre' that spans several different genres.

To do this, just type existing genre names separated by a comma. For example: 'rock, indie, alternative, gospel'. This way, your song will appear in all those different genres simultaneously.

Adding lyrics

With a digital music player, you can easily add or 'embed' lyrics to a song in your library. On some players – such as the latest iPods – these lyrics can be viewed while you're listening on the move.

In Windows Media Player, right-click on a song and select 'Advanced Tag Editor'. Then choose the 'Lyrics' tab. In iTunes, select a song and press Ctrl + I (Mac: Apple + I) to bring up the info on screen. (Alternatively, with the song selected, go up to the File menu and choose 'Get Info'). Select the 'Lyrics' tab and type in the lyrics of your song.

If you can't be bothered to type in all the words, or don't know them, there are loads of lyric sites on the web. Just use your favourite search engine to search for the song title and the word 'lyrics'. Thousands of sites will pop up.

When you've found the lyrics you want, select the words with the mouse and press Ctrl + C (Mac: Apple + C) to copy. Then flip back to the Lyrics screen and press Ctrl + V (Mac: Apple + V) to paste the words.

must know
WMP has a helpful feature; for when you're listening to a random selection of tracks and you really start enjoying tracks by a particular artist and want to hear more immediately. Right-click on the track and from the menu select 'Jump To Artist' or 'Jump to Album' and WMP will take you to another track by the same act.

watch out
When you're creating a genre, be careful with the spelling and the use of spaces. For example, 'Trip hop' will be treated as a completely separate genre to 'TripHop' even though to us they look the same. It will just get annoying and confusing later on if your Library is stuffed with duplicate but misspelt genres.

Skinning in Windows Media Player

One of the best features in Windows Media Player is the ability to change the appearance or the 'skin' of the player. Skins are alternative user interfaces and change the colours and graphics of the player, increase or decrease its size, and move the controls around. They're a lot of fun because they come in all sorts of styles and themes. There is a handful built-in to WMP but there are plenty more to download online. Download them from www.wmplugins.com

1 Make sure Windows Media Player is in what's known as 'Full Mode' (without a skin) by pressing Ctrl + 1 or selecting 'Full Mode' from the 'View' menu.

2 Now bring down the 'View' menu at the top of the screen, and select 'Skin Chooser'.

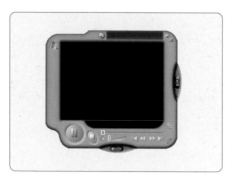

3 A new window will appear with a list of skins on the left and a preview of the new look on the right.

4 Browse through until you find one you like and then click on 'Apply Skin' in the top left-hand corner of the window.

Editing album artwork

When you digitize music from an audio CD, or download music online, the album artwork doesn't get copied along with the tracks. It's useful to learn how to edit the artwork yourself.

Eye-catching covers

When you download music, it's easy to forget that a lot of effort has gone into creating an eye-catching cover. And when you digitize your CDs, there's no simple way of digitizing the cover artwork. However, there is a way each album in your collection can have its correct artwork permanently stored with it.

The solution is to look on the Internet as it is full of album art. Once you've found it, you can add it to your digital music collection really easily in two ways.

iTunes (PC/Mac)

1 In your favourite search engine, search for the album name and the phrase 'album art'.

2 When you've found a suitable image, download the image to your computer (see page 12 for details on how to do this).

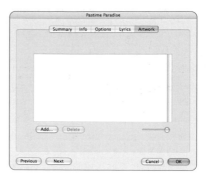

3 A good place to put the image would be in the same folder as the music. On a PC, this is likely to be found in My Documents > My Music. On a Mac, it's just called the Music folder.

4 Flip back to iTunes, group-select all the songs you want to attach to this piece of album art and then right-click on the files (Mac: Ctrl + click). From the revealed menu, choose 'Get Info' and then the 'Artwork' tab.

Manually installing album artwork

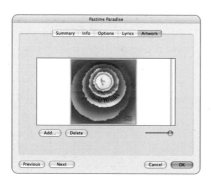

5 If the songs already have album art allocated to them, you'll see it in this window. If not, it will appear blank. At this point either delete the existing art with the 'Delete' button, or add your downloaded image. Those songs now have proper album artwork attached to them.

1 In your favourite search engine, search for the album name and the phrase 'album art'.

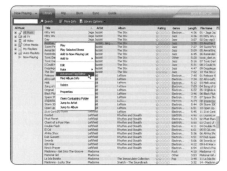

2 When you've found a suitable image, download the image to your computer (see page 12 for details on how to do this).

3 A good place to put the image would be in the same folder as the music. On a PC, this is likely to be found in My Documents > My Music. On a Mac, it's called the Music folder.

4 Launch Windows Media Player. In the Library, right click on the album name you want to edit and select 'Advanced Tag Editor'.

5 When the next window appears, click on the 'Pictures' tab and then click 'Add'. Open the picture you would like to display as album art. Click on 'Open' and that's it.

6 Using player programs

Automatic Album Artwork in Windows Media Player (PC only)

Make sure you're connected to the Internet and launch Windows Media Player.

1 Make sure Windows Media Player is in what's known as 'Full Mode' (without a skin) by pressing Ctrl + 1 or selecting 'Full Mode' from the 'View' menu.

2 Now bring down the 'View' menu at the top of the screen, and select 'Skin Chooser'.

3 A new window will appear with a list of skins on the left and a preview of the new look on the right.

4 Browse through until you find one you like and then click on 'Apply Skin' in the top left-hand corner of the window.

Getting Visual

Beyond music, your player can also generate extraordinary live visuals. Usually referred to as 'visualizers', these built-in pieces of software can be customized in all sorts of clever and wild ways.

The iTunes Visualizer (PC/Mac)

iTunes has a powerful visualizer engine built it. Just hit Ctrl + T (Mac: Apple + T) to turn on the often freaky visual effects. You can also hit the grey 'mandala'-like icon on the bottom right-hand corner of the iTunes screen.

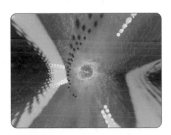

In a relatively short space of time, some animated images will swirl and flow across your screen. The visuals sync to the music playing and will respond in time to beats and frequencies. If you want the visuals to fill the screen hit Ctrl + F (Mac: Apple + F)   press the 'esc' key to flip back again.

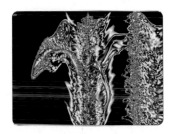

Two good looking visualizations.

Speeding things up

If you've got a powerful computer, the visuals should appear fast-moving and very smooth. However, on a slower computer, or one that's running lots of tasks, the visuals can become jerky and slow. You may need to fine-tune your settings to make them flow faster.

Click the flowery icon in the top-right of the screen to reveal the Visualizer Options dialog box. Experiment with the options to streamline the performance of your visuals.

must know

How slick and smooth your visuals appear will depend on how fast your computer is, and the speed of the computer's graphics card.

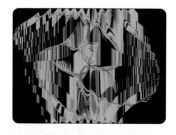

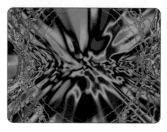

Visualization becoming madder with additional controls.

Controlling the visuals

Another way to affect the visuals is to bring up the 'Basic Visualizer Help' menu. To do this type a question mark (?) using your keyboard and the menu will appear near the top-left of the Visualizer screen. Options such as 'Toggle frame rate capping' and 'Toggle overscan mode' can make your images appear smoother and faster. The others such as 'Display song information' will help you keep track of what's playing.

Ramping it up

After a while, you (and your friends) may get a bit bored of the patterns on offer. Luckily there are some 'hidden' controls built in to spice up the visuals. Just press the 'Z' key to inject something new into the unfolding images. When you've explored that, try pressing 'Q' as well. And, if you would like further variety,you might try hitting the 'A' key from time to time as well.

Download extra visuals

When you've seen everything that can be seen with the iTunes Visualizer, take a trip online where there are masses of free Visualizer plug-ins to download. Sites like soundspectrum.com and itunes.plug-insworld.com have loads on offer with many more being added each week.

Two good places to start:

http://itunes.pluginsworld.com/plugin.php?
directory=apple&software=itunes&category=28
www.apple.com/downloads/macosx/ipod_itunes/

The Windows Media Player - Visualizer (PC only)

To further enhance your listening experience with Windows Media Player, try out the powerful Visualizer. Like iTunes' Visualizer the WMP Visualizer generates graphic displays that change in time with the beat of the music that's being played.

To activate the visual effects, first start a music track playing by double-clicking on a track in the Library screen.

1 Click on the 'Now Playing' tab and you should see a blank screen.

2 Now click on the 'Options' icon just under the 'Now Playing' tab.

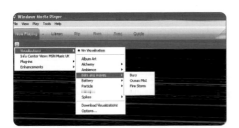

3 Under the 'Visualizations' menu, you'll find a selection of different animations (Alchemy, Bars and Waves, Spikes, etc). Choose one to get started

4 Your screen will fill with your chosen visualization. Use the left and right arrows under the 'Now Playing' window to select different options.

5 To turn off the visuals, right-click in the main window and select 'No Visualization'.

iTunes special moves

As the only player that works with the iPod, iTunes has quickly become one of the most popular and powerful players out there. Apple keep releasing new versions and updating them with better and better features. Here are just a few of them.

Smart searches

Another advantage of digital music players is their powerful search options. In iTunes, type a few keywords into the search box, hit the return key, and you'll see a grey bar appear above your results. By clicking on the words in this bar, you can filter your search results further and further until you arrive at the songs you really want to find. You can also confine your search to different types of music files, podcasts, audiobooks or others.

Party Shuffle

Party Shuffle is a great feature in iTunes. With it you can automatically arrange your favourite and most highly ranked songs into a party playlist. In other words, Party Shuffle is like a normal shuffle playlist, but one that's weighted in favour of the songs you love. Furthermore, unlike a straight shuffle, Party Shuffle gives you much more control over the songs: for example, you can decide what comes next in the list, skip songs, and so on.

To get started, choose 'Party Shuffle' in the left-hand window. A list of your favourite songs will appear with a grey panel at the bottom of the screen. Tick the 'Play higher rated songs more often' box to push more of your favourite songs into the mix.

try this

Make the search bar permanently visible by selecting 'Show Search Bar' under the Edit menu.

Also, if you wish, you can restrict the songs chosen by Party Shuffle to a pre-existing playlist. Try it!

Even more random shuffles

Shuffling is supposed to be random, right? Well, not quite. It isn't known exactly how the shuffle feature in iTunes works, but the more you use the program, the more you may notice the same tunes coming up over and over again. Luckily, though, if you want you can increase the 'randomness' of the shuffle function.

Bring up iTunes 'Preferences' and choose the 'Playback' tab. A screen will appear with a slider labelled 'Smart Shuffle'. Push the slider to the right to decrease the chance of hearing songs by the same artist together, or to the left to increase the chance. Setting the slider in the middle will generate a truly random shuffle.

Playlist Folders

You may find, especially as your digital music collection grows, that your playlist window becomes longer and longer until some of the artists and albums beginning with 'W', 'Y' and 'Z' are screens and screens away. Playlist folders are a great way of avoiding this problem and organizing your playlists.

Create a Playlist Folder by clicking on the 'File' menu and choosing 'New Folder'; give the folder a name. Now you can drag multiple playlists into that folder – all of the Rolling Stones albums, for example, or all your dance mixes, or even lists for particular moods – the choice is yours. Best of all, once you've collected a bunch of playlists in a folder you can play the contents of the entire folder – just select it and all the songs will appear in the main window.

Mac: iTunes > Preferences > Playback.

try this

In the iTunes 'Preferences' screen, under the 'Playback' tab, tick the box next to 'Albums' in the 'Shuffle' menu. Now, instead of songs, iTunes will shuffle entire albums.

Mac iTunes > Preferences > Playback.

Mac: iTunes track information.

Soften the mix

By default, when songs end in iTunes they switch instantly to the next. Sometimes there can even be a gap of a few seconds or more between tunes. A more pleasant listening experience can be achieved, however, if successive songs blend into each other. Here's how.

Bring up the iTunes 'Preferences' screen (under the iTunes menu on the Mac; under the Edit menu on a PC). Select the 'Playback' icon and make sure the tickbox next to 'Crossfade Playback' is ticked. Then drag the slider left or right to decide how many seconds you want the songs to overlap or 'crossfade'. You might want to keep it short, say under four seconds, or the next song may eat into too much of the previous one. Try different values until you're happy with the result.

Changing the beginning and end of a song

Sometimes a song may be too long – it may have an unnecessarily repetitive fade out or a tediously long introduction. Snipping the ending or beginning of a tune is effortless in iTunes.

Select the song you want to edit and right-click the mouse button (Mac: Apple + click). Choose 'Get Info' and then the 'Options' tab. You'll see two options for 'Start Time' and 'Stop Time'. The format is in minutes: seconds: hundredths of a second. So entering 00:13:50 will start a song 13.5 seconds into the track. Similarly, to cut say ten seconds off a four-minute track enter 3:50:00 in the Stop Time (four minutes minus ten seconds). Changing these settings doesn't actually alter the original file at all, so you can go back at any point and restore the original start and end points.

Make songs all the same volume

One of the most annoying things about building a digital music collection is the difference in volume between the songs. Some are quietly recorded, others are massively loud, some have not been digitized properly. The result is often a lot of effort trying to get them all reasonably loud or constantly having to change the volume on your speakers.

The best solution to this is to use the 'Sound Check' function (under Preferences > Playback). Click this box and your music will always play at the same volume.

7 Using your portable player

If you're at all interested in music – and most people are – portable players, such as one of the iPod range, are must-have devices. And they're becoming smaller and more 'feature rich' with every generation. In this chapter, we'll show you how to keep the contents of your portable player and computer in sync. We'll also be outlining some special tips and tricks to bring out the advanced features of your iPod or Zen player.

Advanced portable player

Your portable player is likely to be crammed with all sorts of features to make your music-listening experience as enjoyable and dynamic as possible. Some of these features you may already know about, others you may not.

Mac: iTunes Synchronize window.

Synchronizing

In the digital music world, synchronizing means automatically matching the contents of your computer's music library with that of your iPod or other player. This way you free yourself from having to decide what tracks to put on and what tracks to avoid, which are new – and so on.

When you connect the computer and the player, they talk to each other and synchronize or update their contents. If you've got a top of the range player with plenty of storage space (20 Gb or more), you can probably mirror every single music track on your computer on your player. This is particularly reassuring, because if anything happens to one, you've got the other as backup.

Synchronize an iPod on a Mac

Connect the iPod and allow a few moments for the computer and player to recognize each other. Synchronizing usually happens automatically. If it doesn't, bring up the iTunes menu, choose 'Update songs on iPod' and it will unfold automatically.

Update a Zen player on a PC

Attach the Zen to the PC and wait a few seconds for the computer to recognize the player. If you've

PC: WMP Sychronize window.

installed the Zen software, a browser window with several options will appear. Ignore this and load Windows Media Player and choose the 'Sync' tab.

Turning off synchronization

Sometimes you may not want your computer to dictate exactly what's on your player. If this is the case simply turn off the synchronization feature.

iTunes (PC/Mac)

Just click on the iPod icon on the grey icon shelf at the bottom right-hand corner of the iTunes screen. This will bring up the 'Preferences' screen. Select 'Manually manage songs and playlists'. Now you're in control.

Windows Media Player

With your player connected and Windows Media Player loaded, select 'Options' under the 'Tools' menu and then click on the 'Devices' tab. You should see a list of the CDs, DVDs and portable devices connected to your computer. Highlight the entry for your player on the list and click on 'Properties'. On the next screen, under the 'Synchronize' tab, uncheck the box that reads: 'Start sync when device connects'.

Connecting to a hi-fi or speakers

Modern headphones are good but speakers are better. To connect your player to an amplifier and speakers, you need a special lead – a phono to mini jack lead. The mini-jack goes into the amplifier's headphones' socket. Plug the two phono leads (coded red for the left channel, yellow – or some-

Mac: iTunes 'Preferences' screen.

PC: WMP 'Properties' tab.

must know

Never unplug your player or any other device while it's copying or connected to your computer. You could lose data or damage the device. See page 67 on how to disconnect a player safely.

must know

Some speaker manufacturers now produce speaker systems designed specially for players such as the Zen and iPod. They often come equipped with a digital dock into which the player fits snugly, allowing it to transfer music digitally to the speakers for maximum sound quality.

times black – for the right) into the AUX socket in the back of your amplifier. If you don't know how to do this, it's okay. You won't get electrocuted or anything, but it might be best to ask someone who knows a little bit about hi-fi equipment to do it for you. Then just set your amplifier to AUX and your player's music will play through the speakers.

Both players support different types of graphic equalizer designed to suit different types of music (lounge, piano, jazz, pop, etc.). Some specific settings are also available, which boost the bass, reduce the treble, and so on. Choose one you think will suit what you're listening to.

iPod graphic equalizer

From the 'Main Menu', scroll down to 'Settings' and press the centre button. On the 'Settings' screen, scroll down to 'EQ' (short for 'equalizer') and press the centre button again; you'll be presented with a list of EQ options. Select the option you think is most appropriate and press the 'Menu' button to go back and listen to your newly enhanced music.

Zen graphic equalizer

On the 'Main Menu', scroll down to 'System' and tap the scroll bar. On the next screen, choose 'Audio Settings'. Select 'EQ' and a list of different settings will appear. When you've selected the appropriate setting, press the 'Back' button to step back a menu.

try this

If you want some extra kick in your sound, the Zen has a built-in 'Bass Boost' feature. You'll find it on the 'System' menu under 'Audio Settings'.

Advanced iPod

There's a good reason why the iPod has become the most popular portable music player in the world. Its wonderful interface is full of excellent tricks and clever features to maximize your listening experience.

Updating your iPod

Apple periodically release new updates to the software onboard the iPod. We recommend you check for these at least once a month as they often add features and improve the iPod's performance. These are available at www.apple.com/ipod/down-load/ To install them, download the software (see page 43 to find out to do this) and follow the instructions.

Customizing the Main Menu

The iPod is extremely flexible. You can change many things about it, including the Main Menu. From the 'Main Menu', scroll down to 'Settings' with the click wheel. Press the centre 'Select' button and choose 'Main Menu'. Press 'Select' again and you'll see a list of different aspects of the menu. Turn these on or off by pressing the 'Select' button. When you've finished, press the 'Menu' twice to flip back through to the Main Menu. Your newly chosen menu items will now be visible on the new 'Main Menu'.

Rating songs on the go

If you've used the rating system in iTunes, you'll know how useful it is to be able to grade your collection. But did you know you can also rate the songs on your iPod? When a tune is playing, just press the 'Select' button three times to bring up the rating window, then turn the Click Wheel to increase or decrease the number of stars. Press the 'Select' button to go back to the normal play screen. Best of all, if you synchronize your iPod with your computer, these ratings will be copied back to your music library.

Shuffle

Without doubt one of the most powerful features on the iPod is Shuffle. Normally songs play in the order they are arranged in the playlist, but with Shuffle, the iPod will choose the next song at random – well, more of less at random. To turn this essential feature on, select 'Settings' from the 'Main Menu' then scroll down to 'Shuffle' and centre click it once to turn it on. Your songs will now play in a random, mixed-up order.

Screenlock

The latest iPods have a great security feature called ScreenLock. With ScreenLock you can lock the contents of your player with a personalized four digit PIN code. If someone steals your player or you lose it, you can sleep a bit better knowing that no one will be listening to your music or looking through your photos.

To find this feature, choose 'Extras' from the 'Main Menu' and select 'ScreenLock'. Choose 'Set Combination' first and choose the numbers with the Click Wheel'. Now you'll be given the option to lock the iPod or cancel. If you lock it, you need to type in your four-digit code to unlock the player. Don't forget what your code is. It's best to write it down safely somewhere.

try this

If you're on the 'Settings' screen and changing the 'Shuffle' settings, click it twice until it reads 'Albums'. Now no two songs from the album will play back-to-back.

View album art

By default the album art stored with a song appears as a small icon on the left of the screen. If you want a larger version, press the centre button twice while a song is playing and the artwork will fill the screen. Press the centre button twice more to revert to the smaller view.

On-The-Go

This is a great little feature to create custom playlists on your iPod without having to use your computer. When a great song is playing, hit the centre button and hold it for a count of three. The song will automatically be added to your 'On-The-Go' playlist. You can add as many songs as you like. When you want to listen to this playlist, just scroll down on the 'Main Menu' until you find the 'On-The-Go' option.

Scrubbing

Another excellent aspect of digital music is that you can access any part of it any time. Next time you get bored of a song, try fast forwarding or 'scrubbing' (as it is known in the digital music world).

While the track is playing, press and hold down the arrow buttons on the Click Wheel. A little icon on the screen will bullet forwards or back to show you where you are in the song. In your headphones, you will hear stuttering as the playback moves forwards or back. To restart normal playback, just let go of the Click Wheel.

If your iPod crashes...

If your iPod locks up, freezes or crashes – in other words it no longer responds to any of the buttons

must know

If you lose or forget your PIN code, don't worry. When you next connect your iPod to your computer, it will automatically unlock your iPod. This is because it can recognize that it's your computer.

– it's best to reset your iPod. It's very similar to resetting your computer, and it won't damage any of your music. Think of it as turning the iPod off and then on again.

To reset an iPod:

1) Slide the 'Hold' button to lock (so you can see orange) and then back again.
2) Hold down the 'Menu' button and the centre 'Select' button.
3) Hold them both down until you see the Apple logo appear in the screen.
4) Release the buttons.

Sound Check

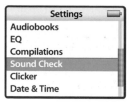

On later iPods, there's a built-in feature to protect your ears. It's usually turned off by default but we recommend you turn it on. There's nothing worse for your ears than a sudden burst of 'Thrash Metal' at an extremely loud volume. You'll find it by choosing 'Settings' from the 'Main Menu', and then locating 'Sound Check'. Press the centre button to turn it on.

Clocks, alarms and stopwatches

Your iPod is not just a music player, it is also a fully-functioning clock, alarm clock and stopwatch. Here's how to get them working:

Date & Time

From the 'Main Menu', scroll to 'Settings' and then to 'Date & Time'. Next choose 'Time In Title'. From now on the current time will permanently sit in the top bar of the main window.

must know

If an older iPod crashes slide the 'Hold' button to lock (orange) and then back again. Now hold down the 'Play/Pause' button and the centre 'Select' button until you see the Apple logo appear on screen.

Alarm Clock

On the 'Main Menu' scroll down to 'Extras' and then choose 'Clock'. Another menu will appear. Choose 'Alarm Clock' and press the centre button to activate it. Scroll down to 'Time' and choose the time you want the alarm to go off at (use the Click Wheel to cycle through the hours and minutes).

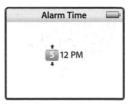

Stop Watch

From 'Extras' on the 'Main Menu', choose 'StopWatch'. Use the centre button to select it, and a fully-fledged stopwatch will fill up the screen. Click 'Start' and you'll notice the buttons change from 'Start and Clear' to 'Pause and Lap'. Yes, you can even store lap times.

Advanced Zen

The Creative Zen players are lightweight and powerful with a host of great features. Like other MP3 players, they make an excellent alternative to the iPod.

Customizing the main menu

The Zen has loads of features and special functions hidden deep inside its software. To make some of these more accessible, or to tune the player more to the way you use it, you can opt to customize the Main Menu.

Select 'System' from the 'Main Menu' and then 'Display Settings' from the next screen. At the top of the screen, you'll see an option to 'Configure Menu'. Click on this and a full breakdown of all the different features of the Zen will appear in a scrollable list. Now just move through them and click to add them to the 'Main Menu'. Click them once more to remove them.

Using the FM radio

The Zen player has a built-in FM radio that automatically tunes into any stations in your area. To activate it, choose 'FM Radio' from the 'Main Menu'. If you haven't configured any stations, the list will be blank. No problem – just press the 'Menu' button and select 'Autoscan'. Your player will scan the airwaves for radio stations and add them to your presets. It takes about a minute.

Once the process is complete, the first station will start playing. Use the left and right buttons to flick forwards and back through the stations. If there's a

station you don't like, quickly press the 'Options'
button and choose 'Delete Preset'. If there's one
you like, you can give it a name it by choosing
'Name Preset'.

Using the voice recorder

If you want to get an idea down quickly or record a
friend's jamming session, try using the Zen's built-in
voice recorder. Select 'Microphone' from the 'Main
Menu', then hit the 'Options' button and start
recording. The status bar at the bottom of the display
indicates how much space you have left on your
player's hard disk.

During recording, you can also hit the 'Options'
button to bring up some controls. Use the 'Pause'
and 'Stop' buttons to control your recording.
Selecting this option will start a new recording in
a fresh file.

Built-In DJ

Another helpful feature on the Zen player is what's
called the 'DJ'. It's an intelligent song-picker with
various options. If you select the 'Music Library'
option on the 'Main Menu' and then scroll down,
you'll find the DJ settings.
- 'Album of the Day' will play the most popular
album of the last 24 hours.
- 'Random Play All' will shuffle all the songs on
your player into a completely random order.
- 'Most Popular' will only play your most
listened-to tracks.
- 'Rarely Heard' will search through your collection
of songs you've barely listened to.

try this
When listening to the
radio, hit the 'Options'
button and choose
'Record Radio'. Nothing
could be easier.

must know
Occasionally, the
manufacturers of the
Zen player, Creative,
release updates of the
player's software (also
known as 'firmware').
The updates correct
bugs and sometimes
add new features.
Remember to check
here periodically to see
if any new firmware is
available:
www.creative. com/
language.asp?sDestUrl=
/support/downloads/
su.asp

Change the wallpaper

If you get bored with the standard colours and backgrounds, why not change them? If you choose 'System' from the 'Main Menu' and then 'Display Settings', you'll find an option to change the 'Theme' – Forest Green, Marine Blue, Sable Black – take your pick.

must know

If your Zen stops responding to your key presses and won't turn on or off, you'll need to reset it. For this you'll need a small, thin object like a paper clip. Quickly insert and remove this object into the reset hole on the bottom of the Zen. Your player will reboot and start working normally.

My ShortCut button

The Zen has four buttons – 'Play/Pause', 'Options', 'Back' and 'My Shortcut'. 'My Shortcut' is a programmable key – like the speed dial button on your mobile phone, you can program the 'My Shortcut' button to link instantly to the major features on the player, such as 'Switch View', 'Start Recording', and 'Album of the Day'. Find the button under 'System > Player Settings' and choose where you want it to lead.

Clock watching

The best place for the Zen's built-in clock is on the main screen. Unfortunately, however, by default, it's hidden. To change this, select 'Clock Settings' from the 'System' screen. Now change the 'Clock In Title' option to 'Digital', and the time will be permanently visible.

Using players as hard-drives

Ever wanted to take some files to work? Or wanted to swap some files with a friend without having to wait to burn them onto CD? Portable music players such as the iPod and Zen don't just work as music players, you can also use them as portable hard drives to store any files you like.

Storage

Most portable players have some kind of built-in storage. The larger-capacity iPods and the Zen have mini hard drives, while players with smaller capacities, such as the iPod nano, have memory stored on a chip. This means they have less storage but are much faster to update and copy files to.

Remember, the more space you use on your player to store files, the less space you'll have for music, videos and photos.

Mac: Using your iPod as a hard drive

To activate the storage properties on your iPod, first connect it to your Mac. Once it appears in iTunes, click on the iTunes icon that appears on the Icon shelf in the bottom right-hand corner. The iPod preferences screen will appear. Under the 'Music' tab you'll see an option 'Enable disk use' at the bottom. Tick this box and the iPod will now appear on your desktop and you can drag and drop files onto it as you would any normal external hard disk.

Mac: iTunes: preferences: music.

PC: Using your Zen as a hard drive

First in the Zen player choose 'Extras' from the 'Main Menu' and then select 'Removable Drive'. The first

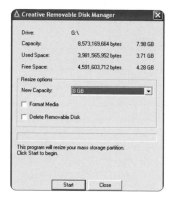

PC: hard-disk utility software.

time you use this feature, you have to decide how much space on your Zen's hard disk you want to dedicate to files. Press the 'Options' key to bring up a selection. Whatever you choose, that portion of the Zen will be formatted to use as a hard disk.

To fill your player with files from a PC, you need to be on the 'Removable Drive' screen before you connect the player to the computer. This is important. You must switch into this mode before you connect it to your PC.

Once connected, it may take a few minutes before the drive is recognized by the computer. Once it is, you can drag and drop files as you wish.

Protect your ears

The Smart volume feature on the Zen player eliminates sudden changes in volume so can protect your ears if you accidentally turn the volume up or a very loud track suddenly comes on. You'll find it off the Main Menu in 'System' and then 'Audio Setting'.

Backing up your music

The hard-drive on your player is a great place to store backups of your digital music collection and protect it from hard-disk crashes and other accidents. Backing up this way is simple. Just connect your player and then navigate to the 'My Music' folder on your PC (or the 'Music' folder if you own a Mac). Then drag this folder onto the icon that represents your portable music player. On the PC, you will find it located under 'My Computer'. On the Mac, you will find it on the desktop.

PC: 'Remove Hardware' screens

Removable hardware

As with all removable hardware – hard disks, digital cameras, players, etc – you should always disconnect them before you unplug the connection cable from your computer.

On a PC, right-click on the 'Remove Hardware' icon in the bottom right-hand corner of your desktop and follow the instructions.

On the Mac, drag the iPod icon onto the wastebasket (don't worry it will be ejected, not trashed). Alternatively you can press Ctrl + click and select 'Eject iPod' from the menu.

want to know more?
• Now that you've learnt the basics about your portable player, why not invest in a set of specialist speakers designed for ipods and other players.

weblinks
• Try Download ilounge. com's free Ipod Book: www.ilounge.com
• To soup up and learn even more about the deep features of your iPod try: www.ipod hacks.com
• Safely backup the contents of your iPod: (Mac) www.amake.us/ software/ipodbackup/
• Download free children's stories for your portable player: http://storynory. com/

8 Photos and videos

The latest generation of portable players have moved beyond just playing music to supporting photo and video playback. Now you can easily slideshow your favourite digital photos and watch an entire film to kill boredom on a long journey. The large disk capacity of some top-of-the-range devices ensures you can store huge amounts of music, pictures and video on them. In this chapter we will show you how to download photos and videos onto your player, where to download great media, and how to watch your favourite films and TV programmes on the move.

Downloading photos

For most of us, digital photography has taken over from conventional film photography, with the result that we may now have hundreds (if not thousands) of photos sitting on our computers.

Storing and viewing photos

Most portable players can now store photos in some capacity. Some will allow you to store pictures but not view them, while others will let you view them on the small screen, and present them as a slideshow on a television (although you may need a special lead to do this – see page 146).

Photo formats

As with digital music, digital photos also use special compression techniques to reduce their size and make them quicker to transfer around the Internet or from computer to computer. And as with digital music this has led to a confusing range of formats that can vary in quality and size.

Luckily, unlike the bewildering digital music formats, all computers and most players can recognize the most popular photo formats. However, there are some minor differences between them that are worth noting.

JPEG (.JPG) – This is the most common format for cameras and pictures online. The amount of compression applied to a JPEG will affect the image quality. At low compression (high quality), the image will be clear and indistinguishable from a printed photo, but the file size will be large. At high compression (low quality), the image may appear fuzzy or 'blocky', but the file size will be small.

TIFF (.TIF) – This is a very high-quality format favoured by some high-end digital cameras. The compression used is 'lossless', meaning no picture information is discarded to make the file size smaller. As a result, TIFF files are large but of a high quality.

RAW – An increasing number of semi-professional (prosumer) cameras now support the RAW format. As it sounds, this format contains no in-camera processing, such as sharpening, colour saturation, etc., and only contains the information caught by the camera's image sensor when the photo was taken. A RAW file will need to be converted to a JPEG before it can be viewed by most players.

GIF – This format is used a lot on the Internet. Its images are limited to 256 colours only as opposed to the 16 million represented by JPEG. That limitation is not really noticeable on artwork, but photos can really suffer.

PNG – These are like high-quality GIF files, but ones that support millions of colours. You may find them here and there on the Internet.

BMP – On a PC, when you save an image from a webpage, it's often saved as a BMP file which is Microsoft's own picture format. It's very high quality.

watch out!
The iPod player supports all these formats, but rival players may not. The Zen Vision for example is only compatible with JPEG files.

Photos from the web

There are literally billions of images on the web and most of them are free for you to use for a non-commercial purpose. Grabbing an image from a website couldn't be easier.

How to grab an image

On a PC, right-click on the image you like and choose 'Save Picture As ...' and then choose a directory you'd like to save the image to. 'My Pictures' folder is a good place.

On the Mac, Ctrl + click on the picture and choose 'Save Image to the Desktop'.

Where to find photos online

Google and Yahoo Image Search

Both these vast search engines allow you to search specifically for images. Enter keywords as you would in a normal search and gallery upon gallery of images will appear. Just click on each individual image to be directed to the website it resides on. From there, if it suits your purposes, you can save it to your hard disk.

Google and flickr homepages.

Yahoo photos webpages and directory.

http://images.google.co.uk

http://images.search.yahoo.com

Flickr.com

Flickr.com is a great site where people share their
photos. You can set up a free account and make your
photos private or public, copy-protected or free for
anyone to use. It's secure, free and effortless to use.
We highly recommend it. As tens of thousands of
users are sharing their images, it's a great place to
find random images, new desktop backgrounds, and
even holiday snaps of countries you may be planning
to visit.

Commercial photo libraries

If you're looking for a specific, high-quality image
and you're prepared to pay for it, you could try one of
the extensive commercial photo libraries online. Run
by established names such as Reuters, Corbis and
Magnum, these sites have millions of images to suit
every possible need. Just search for 'photo library' on
Yahoo.com

try this

PC: If you want to share
the picture you've found
on a website with a
friend, right-click on
the image and choose
'E-mail picture'.

Putting photos on players

With the advent of digital cameras and digital music players that support photos, many people are now choosing to carry a selection or even all of their photos around with them.

must know

It depends on the capacity of your player and the quality of your pictures, but on average you can store about 200 photos for every 1 Gb of storage. So, if your player has 20 Gb storage, that's around 10,000 photos.

Why photos on players?

There are several advantages to having your photos on your portable player. You can access them anywhere you want, whenever you want. At the same time, players such as the iPod can be used for making presentations, which may feature some of your photos.

On holiday, a portable player can help as a backup and a place on which to store photos from a digital camera. Memory cards on digital cameras can get full very quickly and an iPod can act as an excellent temporary storage.

Storing photos on your player is also a great way of making backup copies. Backup is very important for digital photos. The old style printed photos, if looked after, didn't fade too much with age. Nor do digital photo files themselves, but unfortunately CDs do, as do DVDs, hard disks and anything else you might store them on.

Most people today keep all their photos on their computer. If the hard disk fails, or the computer is stolen, those photos are lost forever. Copying them onto your player ensures you have a backup in case of the worst. However, we also recommend you store your photos on CDs or DVDs as well – the more places you keep them, the less likely you are to lose them.

Importing photos on your iPod

iPods are thoroughly photo friendly. You can store upwards of 100 images even on the smallest player in the range.

On a PC

Getting photos from your PC using iTunes is really quite easy. Connect your iPod to your PC and then load up iTunes. Under the 'Edit' menu, select 'Preferences' and then choose the 'iPod' tab in the window that appears. Under 'Photos', you will see you can choose to 'Synchronize' (copy) your photos from the 'My Pictures' folder on your hard disk or from another folder ('Choose Folder...'). Select the folder that contains your photos and then click on 'OK' to start copying.

On a Mac

If you have a Mac, getting photos onto your iPod is a breeze. Just plug your iPod into your computer, wait a few seconds for iTunes to notice it's there and then bring up the 'Preferences' window (either from under the 'iTunes' menu or by clicking on the grey iPod icon on the bottom right). Click on the 'Photos' tab and choose 'iPhoto' from the menu. Then a selection of your photo albums from within 'iPhoto' will appear. You can either decide to synchronize (automatically copy) every single photo or manually copy across the ones you want.

watch out

Copying a lot of photos can take some time, maybe as long as an hour.

try this

To save space on your player, it may be best to sort and organize your photos prior to downloading them. Create a folder called 'New Photos' in your 'My Picture' folder. Copy all your new pics into this and then sychronize just this folder.

Importing photos on your Zen (PC only) - Automatically with sychronization

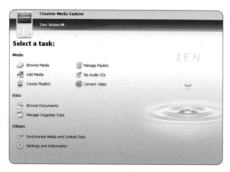

1 With your Zen connected to your PC, select 'Sychronize Media and Outlook Data' on the 'Media Explorer' screen.

2 The 'Creative Sync Manager' will load. You'll see a screen asking you to decide the direction to synchronize in. Leave the settings as they are and hit 'Next'.

3 Choose 'Pictures' and deselect 'Audio'. Click on the 'Next' button to configure the settings.

4 Here, you can select a different directory of photos to synchronize if you have them stored somewhere else. Click on 'Next' when you're done. The sychronization process will commence.

Manually

With your Zen connected to your PC, select 'Add Media' on the 'Media Explorer' screen. In the next screen, browse on your computer to where your photos are stored and select all the images you want to copy over. Click on the 'Add' button and hit 'Next'. The software will take a moment to check the files and then start copying them over. Cleverly, if any of your pictures are not in the required JPG format, 'Media Explorer' will convert them for you.

Putting on a slideshow

Slideshows are a great way to show off your latest holiday pictures, wedding photos or works of art to family and friends – and they're very easy to create.

Slideshows on the iPod

On the iPod, select your photo album and then starting with the first photo hit the centre button. The image will fill the screen. Press the centre button again to bring up the options. Turn the 'TV Off' function to 'Off' and the slideshow will begin. To stop it at any point, just press the 'Menu' button. You can also pause and then restart at any time by tapping the 'Pause' key.

Slideshows on the Zen

On the 'Main Menu', navigate to 'Photos' and then select 'My Pictures'. If you've downloaded any photos to your Zen, you should see a gallery of folders. Choose the one you want and a gallery of thumbnails (small pictures) will fill the screen. Now press the 'Options' button and scroll right down to the bottom of the menu that appears. There you'll see the option 'Start Slideshow'. Click on this to begin a slideshow of your images.

Slideshow on the TV

Of course, the TV is the best place to show a slideshow and with most players displaying full-screen photos on your TV it is effortless.

try this
By default, each slide is set to appear for 3 seconds. If you want them to appear for longer or shorter, choose 'Photos' from the 'Main Menu', and then 'Slideshow Settings'. Clicking the 'Time Per Slide' option will reveal a selection of slide durations from 2 to 20 seconds. Choose the one you want and press 'Menu' to exit.

iPod TV slideshow

When you bought your iPod, you should have received an AV (Audio/Video) cable (smaller iPods such as the iPod nano do not come with a lead). Connect the single end to your iPod's headphone socket and the yellow-coloured plug to the 'Video' socket on your TV or video. If you want sound too, the other two cables – red and white – can be connected to your amplifier or audio inputs on your TV (if you have them).

Once you're hooked up, find the photo album you want to slideshow and press the centre button. A window will appear with a 'TV On' option evident. Scroll down and select this option. Then press the centre button to begin your big screen slideshow.

Zen TV slideshow

With the Zen player, you have to buy a separate special video cable to view your photos on a TV. If you've invested in one, you just need to connect the single end to the AV (Audio/Video) out on the Zen's connector block. Then plug the yellow-coloured plug into the 'Video' socket on your TV or video. Then it's just a case of running a slideshow and your pictures will appear in their full glory on screen.

Transition effects

Pictures in the slideshow usually fade in and out. On the Zen you can use a variety of other effects to bring the pictures in. From the 'Main Menu', select 'System', and then 'Photo/Video' settings. Click on 'Slide Transition' to bring up a list of the special effects on offer, and select the one you want.

Connecting your digital camera

So far, we've looked at downloading photos to your computer and copying them to your player and back again. But it's also possible to bypass your computer altogether and plug your camera directly into your player.

Connecting to your player

Your player is a miniature, portable hard drive with loads of storage space. This storage space can really come into its own when you're using a digital camera out and about – on holiday or when working for example – and you don't want to lug your computer around with you.

Because a digital camera's memory card can fill up quickly, downloading the photos to a portable player is a great way to free up space on the memory card.

Not all players will connect to a digital camera and the ones that do all work slightly differently. Usually, it will be necessary to buy an extra cable or interface to link your player to your camera. If this is a feature you think you will really need, it's probably best to read up on the various players and pick one that has full support for digital cameras.

Connecting your digital camera to an iPod

The iPod is one player that will readily connect to a digital camera. There are two ways to do it but both demand you buy an extra add-on.

Belkin Media Reader

The easiest way is to invest in a Belkin Media Reader for an iPod. It allows your iPod to directly read your digital camera's memory card. They cost about £65, and the reader will recognize most major memory cards including Sony Memory Sticks, SmartMedia, Secure Digital (SD) and Compact Flash – so you should not have a problem with your camera, no matter what the brand. If you are going to be taking a lot of pictures when you are on the move, this may be a good investment.

Belkin Digital Camera Link

This clever gadget allows you to connect your digital camera directly to your iPod. Instead of having to remove the data card, you just connect the camera and iPod together with the Camera Link and a normal USB cable. No special cable is required. It works with most digital cameras. But you might want to check at Belkin's website: www.belkin.com/

Photo and video downloads

If you've transferred photos from your camera onto your player or perhaps have a load of new picstures you've downloaded elsewhere, at work or school, for example, it's easy to then move them from your player to your computer at home. It's also easy to download video these days. Over the next few years, more and more video and TV programmes will be available to download from the Internet.

Copying photos from your player (PC/Mac)

Using an iPod

First launch iTunes on your computer and make sure 'Enable disk use' is enabled for your iPod. Visit the 'Preferences' screen and under the 'Music' tab you'll see a check box for this function.

Now, your iPod should appear on your desktop as a hard disk. Click on it to open and browse the folder labelled DCIM. Select the photos you want to copy to your computer.

Mac: iTunes photo preferences.

Using a Zen

Connect your Zen to your PC and wait for the 'Creative Media Explorer' to appear. Choose 'Browse Media' from the menu. You'll see your player's icon in the left-hand side of the screen. Click on the plus (+) sign next to its icon to reveal the directories on the player. Click on 'Pictures' and the various photo folders on your player will be revealed. To copy them, drag and drop them onto your desktop.

Creative media explorer.

watch out!
On the iPod you should see a folder named DCIM; your photos are in there. On other players, the location may differ.

must know
Podcasts are shows that you can subscribe to and download. Some are just radio programmes, others, video podcasts (sometimes referred to as vodcasts), feature video clips, including news shows, documentaries and other programmes. You can subscribe to podcasts so that they download automatically whenever they are released. See page 32, for instructions on how to download a video.

Import photos from your iPod using iPhoto (Mac only)

If you've got an Apple Mac, you're lucky – you can use iPhoto, a great program for managing all your pictures. Just connect your iPod to your computer and click on the 'Import' icon at the bottom of the screen. (Note: there are several versions of iPhoto so the import icon may be in different places. If in doubt, press Apple + O to bring up the 'Import' screen.) Your pictures should now import into your album.

Import photos using Photoshop Album (PC only)

Photoshop Album is a great program for organizing photos on the PC – and it can import directly from the iPod and other players. Here's how. Connect your player to your PC and then open Photoshop Album. Under the 'File' menu, you'll find an option called 'Organizer'. Select this and then choose 'Get Photos' and choose your player as your import directory.

Downloading video

Faster Internet connections, bigger hard disks and portable video players have all contributed to a massive rise in video downloading from the Internet. Today, websites offer hundreds of free clips and entire programmes to download. In some countries TV programmes are available to download at the same time as they are being broadcast on TV.

Furthermore, an increasing number of portable players are supporting video playback. The iPod led the way, but the rest are following suit. Some people now download their favourite programmes or record them on a Personal Video Record like a TiVo and then transfer them onto their players to watch on the commute to work. The good news is, you won't be left out. If you've already got a portable player that plays video, you're already part of the future.

Where to find video online

The number of video sites is increasing by the day.

Google and Yahoo video

The two biggest search engines in the world both run their own dedicated video download sites. Many clips are free, while some demand a small sale price before you can download them.
http://video.search.yahoo.com/
http:///video.google.com

YouTube

This is a very popular video-sharing site where anyone and it seems everyone can upload and download anything they want. It has a really powerful and easy-to-use interface and a whole host of funny clips and short films.
http://www.youtube.com/

iTunes Music Store

If you want videos for your iPod, this should be the first place to start looking. You can choose from over 2,000 music videos, several popular TV shows, and even some full-length films.

must know
Video files are big – much bigger than music or photo files. And unfortunately, video files also come in a bewildering array of different formats. Refer to our guide on pages 32-8 for all you need to know about downloadable video.

Videos on a portable player

It's hard to imagine that just a couple of years ago, it was virtually impossible to download an entire feature film. Now you can watch films on your portable player while travelling.

Watching videos on your Zen (PC only)

The Zen supports a very broad range of video formats: all the MPEGs, 1, 2 and 4, and Windows Media Video (WMV), the Microsoft standard for video on the PC. (For a more detailed explanation of video formats, see pages 34–5).

They can also be any length and any picture size. The player will shrink them automatically to fit the player's screen.

Watching videos on your iPod (PC/Mac)

The iPod is very particular about the video files it will play. It only likes MPEG 4 and what's known as H.264 video, which is a new, high-quality format developed by Apple. So you're restricted to only watching videos compressed in those formats. Of course, all the videos downloadable from the iTunes Music Store are iPod-ready but you have to pay a charge. In addition, many free sites that offer video – Google Video, for example – now offer their clips in iPod-ready format. Alternatively, you can convert your existing videos to iPod-friendly formats. See below.

To download video onto your Zen:

1 Connect your player to your PC and wait for the Creative Media Explorer software to open.

2 Next, choose 'Add Media'. This launches the Import Wizard which will copy files to your Zen.

3 On the next screen, select the videos you want in the browser screen on the left. Then click on 'Add' to add them to the queue on the right.

4 Hit the 'Next' button and the files you have chosen will be copied.

8 Photos and videos

5 Safely disconnect your Zen player, and browse to 'Videos' on the 'Main Menu'.

6 In 'Videos' on the next menu click the file names of your video files to start watching.

How to get video onto your iPod using iTunes.

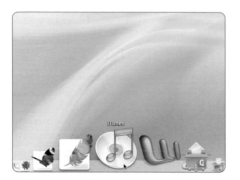

1 Connect your iPod to your computer and open iTunes. If you have sychronization on, any videos in your iTunes will automatically be copied onto your iPod.

2 If you've turned sychronization off, browse to the video folder in the 'Playlist' window on the left.

3 With the mouse, drag and drop the videos you want to watch on your iPod onto the iPod icon.

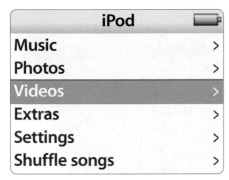

iPod	
Music	>
Photos	>
Videos	>
Extras	>
Settings	>
Shuffle songs	>

4 On the main menu of your iPod, choose 'Videos' and then select a video you want to watch.

1:40   -2:35

5 Choose 'TV off' and then the video will start playing.

want to know more?

• Once your player is full of photos, you can treat them like music files – open them, rate them, and best of all, show them to friends and family in the form of a slideshow.
• The iPod has a permanent directory called 'Photos' which doesn't actually contain your photos. Ignore it.

weblinks

• The easiest way to convert video files to iPod format is to use Apple's Quicktime program: www.apple.com/quicktime
• Convert your DVDs to iPod format (PC/Mac) – Cucusoft DVD to iPod Converter: www.cucusoft.com/
PQ DVD to iPod Video Converter: www.pqdvd.com/
Movkit DVD to iPod Ripper: www.movkit.com/
• Convert YouTube videos into iPod format with TubeSock (Mac) www.stinkbot.com/ Tube sock/index.html

9 Podcasting

There's a big buzz about podcasting at the moment. A Podcast is an Internet radio show you can subscribe to. Instead of having to tune in when the show is on, your computer automatically downloads a new episode. In this chapter we'll explain the ins and outs of podcasting and how to find the best examples online. And, because anybody can make them and produce them for a potential audience of millions of people worldwide, we've even included a guide to 'Making your own podcast'. The world awaits your message ...

Getting started with podcasts

Podcasts are the latest revolution in radio. They are internet radio shows you can subscribe to. Once you've signed up, a podcast feed tells your player when a new episode or show is available and your player then downloads it.

The future of radio

Using a unique subscription method, podcasts mean you don't have to be around at a certain time to catch your favourite show. You can listen to it whenever you like. And, because it's downloaded to your computer, you can copy it to your player or burn it onto CD and then listen to it wherever and whenever you like.

Many commercial broadcasters are launching podcast versions of their shows. They believe this subscribe-and-download way of listening is the future of radio and may even take over the traditional 'broadcasting' model. So podcasting is here to stay.

Finding podcasts online

There are hundreds, even thousands, of podcasts available on the Internet today, covering all possible subjects from music to TV to politics to food. Here are some of the best places to look.

Apple Music Store

Unsurprisingly, Apple's iTunes Music Store is currently the number one place to look for all the top-rated podcasts on the web. There's a vast range of subject matter, but the quality is variable. Visit www.apple.com/

BBC Radio website.

BBC

The BBC have started making a lot of their shows available in podcast form: interviews, overseas reports, current affairs and 'Best of ...' versions make great downloads. Visit www.bbc.co.uk/radio

Newspapers

Most major newspapers are experimenting with some form of podcasting, converting their articles into audio or having their correspondents host investigation programs or chat shows.

Podcast sites

Many directory websites have sprung up to index the podcasting revolution. Some of the best places to start looking are:

www.podcast.net/

http://podcasts.yahoo.com/

www.podnova.com/

http://ipodder.org/

must know

Because anyone can make and publish a podcast, there's little in the way of quality control on the web. Many of the shows are of poor production quality or they just ramble. To avoid disappointment, try to download only highly rated shows from good quality outlets such as the iTunes Music Store.

Apple Music Store, http://podcasts.yahoo.com

Downloading podcasts

Getting a podcast of your favourite radio show is a two-step process. First you subscribe and then you download an episode (or episodes if the show has an archive). You can either let your computer do this automatically or you can do it yourself manually.

Subscribing to a podcast in iTunes automatically (PC/Mac)

1 Bring up the iTunes Music Store by clicking on the green icon in the left-hand panel.

2 Click on the 'Podcasts' link in the left-hand box on the homepage.

watch out!

The majority of podcasts are free, however, some do charge a small subscription fee. If you are in any doubt, read the small print.

3 The 'Podcasts' home page will load. Browse it until you find a podcast that interests you.

try this

If you click the grey arrow next to the podcast name, all the available episodes for the show will be revealed. Those in grey are yet to be downloaded. Black ones can be played straight away.

4 Click on the link for the show to see its homepage, then hit the 'Subscribe' button.

5 iTunes will ask you if you definitely want to subscribe. Answer 'Yes' (you can unsubscribe later if you want to).

6 The latest episodes will begin to download in the iTunes 'Podcast' window. An orange icon indicates that a podcast is being updated.

must know

If it's all getting too much, then you may want to discontinue downloading a show. Just highlight its name in the iTunes 'Podcast' window and then click on the unsubscribe icon.

Manual subscription

Sometimes, while browsing the web, you'll come across websites with links to their own podcasts. These may not automatically trigger iTunes to subscribe to the podcast for you. Instead, you will need to subscribe manually.

Subscribing to a podcast manually with iTunes (Mac/PC)

1 In your web browser, open the podcast page and click on the podcast link.

2 Highlight the whole address in the space at the top of the browser where the link appears and copy it by pressing Ctrl + C (Mac: Apple + C).

3 Switch to the iTunes 'Podcast' screen and under the 'Advanced' menu, choose 'Subscribe To Podcast'.

4 Paste the weblink into the box provided (use Ctrl + V on the PC, or Apple + V on the Mac) and click 'OK'. You're now subscribed to the podcast, and the shows will download automatically for you.

Unfortunately, Windows Media Player does not have support for podcasts built in, so you have to download a free program called 'Doppler' to handle the podcasts for you.

try this

It's a good idea to create a separate folder called 'Podcasts' in your 'My Music' folder.

Subscribing to a podcast manually with Windows Media Player (PC only)

1 Download 'Doppler' from www.doppler radio.net and double-click on the Doppler file to install it

2 During the installation, point the program to the 'Podcasts' directory you created earlier in your 'My Music' folder'

3 In your web browser, navigate to a page with a podcast you want to subscribe to on it.

4 To copy the podcast's address or 'feed', right click on the 'RSS subscription' link and choose 'Copy Shortcut' from the menu.

9 Podcasting

5 Open Doppler and click on 'Add Feed'. Press Ctrl + V to paste the address in the box labelled 'URL'.

6 To start downloading episodes, click the 'Retrieve Now' button.

7 Once the files have downloaded, load Windows Media Player and click on 'My Playlists' in the Library window.

8 You should see a playlist with the same name as your podcast show. It contains all your freshly downloaded radio shows.

must know

You can subscribe to as many podcasts as you want but remember that podcasts are usually much longer than songs and so take up far more storage space. Fifty shows, for example, are going to take up a great deal of storage space.

Managing your podcasts

It's important to keep a regular check on your podcasts. The downloaded files can quickly fill disk space. And, as most podcasts produce new episodes weekly or even daily, you can soon develop a backlog.

In iTunes, click on the 'Settings' button in the bottom right-hand corner of the screen. The options here will help you streamline your podcast habit. The 'Keep' setting is worth adjusting if you're low on disk space as it determines how long a podcast remains on your computer before it's deleted.

Copying podcasts to your iPod with iTunes (PC/Mac)

By default all your latest podcasts will be copied to your iPod as soon as you synchronize it with your computer. If you want to be more selective, bring up the 'Preferences' (under the 'Edit' menu on a PC, or the 'iTunes' menu on Mac). Under the 'Podcast' tab you'll find the option 'Automatically Update Selected Podcasts Only'. Flick this on and then only tick the checkboxes next to the shows you want copied to your iPod.

Another way to retain full control is to simply drag and drop the shows you want on your iPod from the 'Podcast' window onto the iPod icon in iTunes.

Once the shows are on your iPod, just choose 'Podcasts' from the main menu and you'll soon be on your way to radio heaven!

Copying podcasts to other players via Windows Media Player

If you have already downloaded podcasts into Windows Media Player, transferring them to your player is easy. Just right-click on the podcast in the 'Library' window and choose 'Add to Sync List ...' from the menu. The next time you connect your player to your PC, your chosen podcast – and any other podcasts and files you have added to the synchronize list – will be automatically copied to your player.

Making your own podcasts

Recording, editing and publishing a podcast is remarkably easy – the tens of thousands of podcasts already online is testament to that. With just a few free and simple tools you too can be up and broadcasting your thoughts, observations and ideas to a potential audience of millions.

What you need

The great thing about audio recording and production is that you don't need an expensive, powerful computer. Most modern PCs can effortlessly handle audio production. They will happily record any signal coming in, give you enormous editing power, and export your final cut to a digital music file and publish it on the web as a podcast file.

must know

Make sure you have enough disk space in advance. Audio recorded directly into your computer is uncompressed, which means it takes up a lot of space – usually around 10 Mb a minute, compared to 1 Mb a minute for an MP3 file. In other words your 30-minute talk show will take up around 300 Mb on your hard disk.

A microphone

The microphone is the most important part of the recording process. The quality and impact of your show is directly linked to the quality of your recorded voice – and that means getting a good microphone. If you're going to spend money experimenting with podcasting, spend it on a microphone.

Many computers and laptops have built-in microphones. If you can avoid using these, do. They're usually average quality and will pick up any background noise, including the telephone and television, chairs creaking, even the hum of your computer.

The best type of microphone is a USB one. These plug straight into your computer and provide high-quality digital sound. They work on both Macs and PCs and are usually inexpensive. Many feature noise-cancelling elements which can filter out background noise while you're recording.

Alternatively, you can use a normal 'analogue' microphone, which has a small headphone-like socket at the end (a 3.5mm jack). This simply plugs into your soundcard or the audio-in socket on your computer.

Headphones

Headphones are another useful item to have – the quality, however, isn't as important as with the microphone. Headphones allow you to monitor the quality of your voice, that's both sound quality and tonal quality. Plus you can scan for any background noise that might interfere with your recording.

Recording and editing software

There's all sorts of audio software available today, professional and amateur, at a range of prices. However, before spending any money try Audacity, a free program that works on both PC and Mac. You can use it to record, edit, and add effects and it's really simple to use; download it from http://audacity. sourceforge.net. We'll be using it for the project on how to make your own podcast on page 168.

Ready to record

Connect your microphone and headphones to your computer and launch Audacity. Click on the big red record icon (or press R on your keyboard) and recording starts. You'll see chunks of your recording appear as the seconds go by. Remember to turn off

must know

It seems obvious but the best podcasts are well-structured, entertaining and, most importantly, about something. If you want an audience for your podcast, you need to make a plan. What is your podcast about? What do you want to say? Make some notes in advance, prepare any interviews and write a rough script. Off-the-cuff shows are great but unless you're a professional broadcaster they're very hard to pull off.

any music you might be playing on your computer or that will be recorded, too.

Check levels

It's very important that your signal is not too quiet or too loud. Too quiet and you risk allowing lots of background noise, hiss and hum into your audio. Too loud and you can cause distortion and static – which is very unpleasant to listen to. The best way to check the levels is to record a test track.

● Open a new Audacity window by pressing Ctrl + N (Mac: Apple + N), and select 'Record'.

● Speak as loudly as you can without shouting.

● Lower the input volume if necessary or move away from the computer.

● Watch the volume indicators. Ideally, you want them to reach the three-quarter mark when talking normally, pushing up close to the end when you get a bit more 'animated'.

 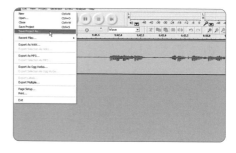

The Audacity interface.

Record

Once you've selected 'Record' start talking. Don't worry about pauses or mistakes, as you can always cut these out later. Just stream away and see what comes out. Your 'Record' screen will fill with mountains and troughs – this is your digital audio recording.

To avoid getting feedback when recording, disconnect your computer from your speakers, and make sure you're wearing headphones instead.

Pause and regroup

If you lose track of what you're saying or need to reorganize your thoughts, just hit the blue 'Pause' button (or press the P key on your keyboard). When you're ready to continue, hit the 'Pause' button again and the recording will continue from where you left off.

Stop

When you've completed the recording, select the 'Stop' button (or press the S key or spacebar on your keyboard). Scroll through the peaks and troughs of your recording – the higher the peaks, the louder the signal. A straight line represents silence or a very quiet signal. Use the plus and minus zoom controls to take a closer look (see 'Editing your Podcast' on page 170).

The best thing to do at this stage is save your file. Select 'Save Project As' under the 'File' menu and choose where you want to save it.

must know

If you want to record some extra bits for your show or an entire new take, select 'New Recording' under the 'File' menu. When a new window appears, just repeat the record process again.

Editing your podcast

Editing is really the fun part of podcasting. Digital audio gives you power over your recording – it's a real joy to cut, splice and rework the sound. Plus you get your own radio show at the end.

must know

If you get lost at any point when zooming in or out, hit Ctrl + 2 (Mac: Apple + 2) to flip back to a normal level of zoom.

Sound waves

Every recording you make with Audacity will appear on screen as sound waves. These can be edited in very much the same way as you edit words in a word processor. Sections can be cut out, moved or repeated. Bad takes can be cut, and music and separate recordings can be inserted at any point.

Zooming in and out

The 'Zoom' function in Audacity will let you get deep into the detail of your recording – the best place to perform precise cuts. To zoom in, either click on the magnifying glass icon with a plus in it or press Ctrl + 1 (Mac: Apple + 1). To zoom out, press Ctrl + 3 (Mac: Apple + 3).

Cutting a segment

To perform a cut, highlight the section you want to trim by dragging the mouse over the area. Don't worry if you don't get it exactly right first time, just drag again until you're satisfied you've highlighted the area you want.

Fine-tune the edges of your cut by moving the mouse pointer to the ends of the selection. The pointer will change to a white hand, and you can then click and drag to move the point forwards or back.

Press the spacebar to audition the area you've selected and adjust the beginnings and end accordingly. To cut the section, press backspace, or alternatively Ctrl + X (Mac: Apple + X). The latter action allows you to paste it elsewhere in the recording.

Undoing

After deleting or editing, if you cut the wrong part or decide you want to keep the section, no problem. You can simply undo the cut by pressing Ctrl + Z (Mac: Apple + Z) or by choosing 'Undo' under the 'File' menu. Alternatively, click on the curved arrow icons.

Audacity features multiple 'undos', meaning you can track back as far as you like through all your actions. This way if you made a big mistake earlier during the editing you can keep pressing or selecting 'Undo' until you reach the point where it all went wrong – and start again.

Trim outside section

Sometimes you might want to keep a small part of a recording and delete the rest. No problem. Select the area you want to keep and click on the 'Trim Outside Selection' icon. The rest of your recording will be wiped with the part you liked left intact.

To get an instant overview of your entire recording, first select the entire file first by pressing Ctrl + A (Mac: Apple + A) then click on the 'Fit Selection',

Fade away

To get a professional-sounding fade effect, select the area to which you want to apply the fade. Then under the 'Effects' menu select 'Fade In' or 'Fade Out'.

Import another recording

If you want to insert a music file or an audio snippet you previously recorded, place the cursor where you want the new file to appear and then choose 'Import Audio' under the 'Project' menu. The new audio will appear in your timeline.

must know

If you're unsure of exactly what you've been doing, bring up the 'History' window. You can find it under the 'View' menu and it lists every single edit, action and delete you've performed on the file. Click on any action to switch back to that point in time.

Final touches

Once you have edited your podcast recording and are completely happy with the result, it's time to prepare the file for Internet broadcast.

Processing

The first task is to process the sound file to make sure that it is sufficiently loud and at the highest sound quality. This process is known as 'normalization'.

1. Select the entire file by pressing Ctrl + A (Mac: Apple + A).
2. Under the 'Effects' menu, choose 'Normalize'.
3. In the window that appears, leave all the boxes ticked and click OK.

The process may take some time if you have a large file, but when it's finished, your podcast should sound consistently loud.

Under the 'Effects' menu, choose 'Normalize'.

Editing the podcast information

Any file uploaded to the Internet should have detailed tag data attached to it. This includes podcasts. Tags let search engines and users understand exactly what your file is, who made it and how to classify it.

   To enter this information in Audacity, select the 'Project' menu and choose 'Edit ID3 tag info... '. A window will pop up with various fields to fill in. Enter the correct information – and watch for spelling mistakes. Now, wherever your file ends up, listeners will know who recorded it and be directed to your website (if you have one).

Exporting

Okay, now you're ready to export your file from Audacity. Under the 'File' menu, you will see a couple of Export options.

Export as WAV file

This will spit out a self-contained, uncompressed version of your podcast in WAV format. WAV is the highest quality audio format on the PC (although Apple computers can read these files as well). Since it is uncompressed, it has very high audio quality but the files are too big to share on the Internet. However, if you want to keep a pristine version of your podcast (maybe for editing in the future) this is the format to export in.

We recommend that you export your podcast as a WAV file first and then compress the file into an Internet-ready format in a separate program like iTunes (see below).

Export as MP3

MP3 is the format of choice for sharing digital audio on the Internet. Unfortunately, you will have to download and install the LAME MP3 Encoder to use this function in Audacity. You'll find the software and detailed instructions on how to install it here: http://audacity.sourceforge.net/help/faq?s=install&item=lame-mp3

Compression

Podcasts have to go through a compression process before they are uploaded onto the Internet. As discussed earlier, a raw digital audio file is far too big

Select the 'Project' menu and choose 'Edit ID3 tag info.'

for people to download easily from the web. Instead, the files must be compressed into MP3 format. This makes them a tenth of the original size without losing any sound quality.

For an explanation of all the different file compression formats, see page 15.

Compressing in iTunes (PC/Mac)

Open the file in iTunes, select it and then, under the 'Advanced Menu', choose 'Convert Selection to MP3'. iTunes will then create a new, compressed version of your file which will appear in the library.

Compressing a podcast in Windows Media Player (PC only)

Open the file in iTunes, select it and then, under the Advanced Menu, choose Convert Selection to MP3. iTunes will then create a new, compressed version of your file which will appear in the Library.

watch out!

You have to have an account with the iTunes Music Store to be able to upload a podcast onto their system

Going 'live'

In order for other people to be able to listen to your podcast, you have to first upload it to a particular location on the Internet. Then you create a weblink or 'feed' so people can find it. You'll have to use an FTP program (see page 14) to upload the file somewhere where others can download it – a friend's website, for example, or the free webspace your web provider may give you with your account. There are also websites that will host your podcast for free.

Try www.ourmedia.org. Wherever you end up putting it, make a note of the address – this address

will become an essential part of your podcasts 'feed'.

Using iTunes, load up the iTunes Music Store and click on the 'Podcasts' link in the left-hand column. Enter the address of your podcasts and click 'Continue'. The store will then automatically generate a page for your podcast.

It's no good spending hours making a polished broadcast if no one is going to listen to it. Luckily there are loads of free channels in which to tell people about your new opus. Any of the big podcast directories will take new feeds or you can visit the popular podcast site www.feedburner.com.

want to know more?

• Look out for an EXPLICIT tag alongside the file name of a podcast. It's there to flag possible adult themes, harsh language or material that is inappropriate for children.

weblinks

• Promote your podcast online: http://pod casting.about.com/od/p romotingyourpodcast/
• To find good podcasts, use a special search engine: http://podcasts.yahoo. com/ or http://podscope.com/
• Alternatively, rifle through a directory www.podcastbunker. com/ www.podcastalley.com/

10 Mobile phones and other devices

It's not just computers that you can download to. Phones, video games consoles and even video recorders can now share and download media. Usually, whatever you download onto these devices can be transferred onto a computer or portable player. In this chapter, we'll introduce you to some easy ways to download onto your phone and show you how to get started downloading onto other devices.

Downloading to mobile phones

Ringtones, pictures, video clips, games, music tracks – there's lots to download onto your phone these days. Ringtones are the most popular media to download, but increasingly music tracks and even videos are being offered by mobile phone companies.

How to download to your phone

There are two ways to download media onto your phone – by text message or by mobile Internet. If your phone is less than two years old, there's a very good chance that it supports mobile Internet access (also known as WAP). If it's older, you'll probably have to download via text message.

To download from a mobile website, either enter the web address into your phone or use your phone's Internet browser to navigate to the web address.

Alternatively, some companies will offer to send you a weblink via text. In this case, you usually text a code word ('GO' for example) to a specific number. The computer at the other end then replies to your text with a 'Wap push' or 'Service message'. When you open this message, you are directed straight to your download online.

Ringtone and wallpaper downloads

Wallpapers come in a standard format and are compatible with all phones. Ringtones, however, come in two main formats. Polyphonic can play many notes simultaneously so they sound very much like the original song and pleasant to the ear. Truetones are digitally recorded and sound like their source – be it a sound effect or a voice recording.

The best place to find tones and wallpapers is online. Your network's own website will sell them, as will a slew of independent retailers.

Once you've found a download you want, you'll be asked to text a special number with the download code for your chosen purchase. For example, you may need to text 'tone rollingstones' to 948 to order a Rolling Stones ringtone. A few seconds later, you'll receive a text message back either containing the ringtone or a link to the tone on a mobile internet site so you can download it.

Downloading music tracks

Most phones now function as portable music players and many of the major mobile networks offer their own music shops so you can download music to your phone no matter where you are.

Typically, though, you need to install special software on your phone to allow you to buy and download tracks. Purchased music is often locked to your handset and heavily copy protected. If you transfer it to your computer or to a portable player, it probably will not play.

Transferring music onto your phone

Most recent phones will play music tracks in MP3 format, so you may be able to upload digital music from your computer. If you've opted for different formats for your music (Apple's AAC or Microsoft's WMA, for example), then most networks offer 'track converter' software. This will convert your songs, transfer them to your phone, and keep the contents of your phone and your music library synchronized. A lot of 'track converter' software only works on the

try this
If you're going to be doing a lot of downloading on your phone, it may be wise to invest in a monthly download bundle rather than paying for each download. These are offered by most networks and give you a certain amount of download access (4 Mb, 10 Mb etc.) each month for a fixed price

PC. If you own a Mac, you may not be able to transfer music onto your phone, unless you own a fully compatible Motorola iTunes phone.

Watching video on your phone

Videos for mobile phones download via the mobile Internet in much the same way as music tracks.

As ever, file formats can be a problem. Most video phones will play simple MPEG 1 or 2 files, but many will balk at playing QuickTime movies and clips encoded in DIVX or MPEG 4 (see pages 34-5).

If you're using your phone to buy and download clips from commercial networks, it is important to consider download speed. If you're using a second-generation phone with GSM technology, your connection to the Internet may be too slow for you to fully enjoy video downloads on your handset. At the same time, you'll probably be paying a per-second or per-megabyte charge for every download you make.

If you have a third-generation or 3G phone, your connection speed is much faster, closer to that of broadband. This makes downloading music and video as much as ten times quicker and cheaper. Many 3G networks also offer streaming TV stations.

Downloading games and programs

Games and small programs, such as alarm clocks, are often written in a computer language called JAVA, so your phone will need to be JAVA-enabled for them to work. They are downloaded in the same way as ringtones and wallpapers, and are usually saved in the 'Applications' or 'Games' menu. Downloads may be saved to your phone's memory card as well.

watch out!

Mobile networks may charge you for both the game you've downloaded and the time you spend on the Internet downloading it. If the game has Internet features – such as an online hi-score chart and chat, for example – you will probably also be charged to access those features.

Personal Video Recorders (PVRs)

PVRs are video recorders with built-in hard disks that can record TV programmes in digital quality. They often allow you to pause live TV and strip out the advertisements.

Digital recording

Also known as Hard Disk Recorders and Digital Video Recorders, PVRs are the latest hi-tech incarnation of a video recorder. Rather than recording onto tape or DVD, they digitize TV programmes directly to disk. This gives you much higher quality than tape, and allows you to record far more. It depends on the manufacturer but most PVRs can record on average between 30 and 60 hours of TV.

Many are also fitted with Electronic Program Guides, which give you an onscreen listing of the TV schedules. You can use this to tick the shows you want to record in advance. You can also tag series to record each week or each month so you never miss a show.

Top of the range models

These PVRs come fitted with internal DVD burners that enable you to burn your favourite TV programmes onto compact disc. This way you can build up an archive of your favourite shows, free up space on the PVR's hard disk and share programmes with friends.

With some brands of PVR you can access and copy recorded TV shows onto your computer – and from there onto your portable player.

try this

If you've got a PC and you want to store TV programmes digitally, you may want to consider a PVR add-on for your computer. These turn your PC into a fully functioning PVR with the added advantage of being able to download episodes to portable players such as the Creative Zen.

Downloading to the Xbox 360

The Microsoft Xbox 360 is a powerful games console –
technologically it's like a small, high-performance computer
and will happily play music and video.

More than a games console

The Xbox 360 is a great piece of hardware. Not only
can owners play state-of-the-art video games and
watch DVDs, they also connect to the Internet
and download music and other media to its built-in
hard disk.

Despite its Internet connection, you cannot
actually browse websites and check your email with
the Xbox 360. All connections to the Internet are
handled through its 'Dashboard' interface, which
limits you to downloading games demos and
updates and connecting to the Xbox live community.

Listening to your own music on the Xbox 360

One powerful feature the Xbox does support,
however, is the ability to rip CDs and read music files
so that you can transfer your music onto the Xbox's
internal hard drive. This way you can listen to your
own music while you're playing games. There are
three easy ways to do this.

Ripping a CD to the Xbox

Insert an audio CD into the Xbox 360 and the 'Music
Player' application will pop up and start playing the
CD. Navigate to the 'Rip CD' button and tick the songs
you would like to copy to the Xbox's hard drive.

Connect your player to the Xbox

If you've got a Zen, an iPod or similar portable player, you can connect it directly to the Xbox via a USB cable. After a short delay, the Xbox will automatically recognize the player as an external hard drive. You can then use it as a jukebox and access individual tracks and playlists via the 'Dashboard' interface.

While you can connect an iPod to an Xbox 360, you cannot view any of the pictures stored on the player, nor can you listen to copy-protected music tracks bought from the iTunes Music Store.

Streaming music from your PC

Linking your games console and your computer is a great way to get the best from both. You can use your Xbox as a Media Centre to stream the music, videos and photos from your computer onto your TV.
• Download Windows Media Connect (WMC) from the official Xbox website: www.xbox.com/pcsetup
• Make sure your PC and your Xbox are linked with a network cable.
• Open the Media window on your Xbox 'Dashboard'. Select 'Music' and then 'Computer'.
• A list of all compatible local computers will appear.
• Choose your PC and a list of albums, playlists and songs will appear. Select and start playing.

Viewing photos on the Xbox

Portable players are not the only devices you can connect to an Xbox. The console will view photos from digital cameras and read files from portable hard drives. Connect your camera to your Xbox via a USB cable, then, in the 'Media' panel, select 'Pictures' and then 'Camera'. Your images will then appear.

must know

The standard Xbox only has an 8 Gb hard disk. While that's enough for an impressive 1,920 songs, it will soon fill up, especially if you are also downloading games and games demos from the Internet.

Downloading to the PSP

Sony's PSP (PlayStation Portable) is a high-powered video games console. However, it does much more – allowing you to watch downloaded films or listen to downloaded music.

watch out!

The PSP will only play MP3 files and Sony's own ATRAC3 format. It will not play Windows Media Audio (WMA) or Apple's iTunes songs in AAC format.

PSP memory

The PSP doesn't have a built-in hard drive but instead uses a memory stick similar to those used in digital cameras. The PSP memory card is of a very specific type, however, known as a Sony Memory Stick Duo or Pro Duo. There are other Sony memory sticks but none of these are compatible with the PSP.

The PSP comes with a bundled 32-Mb memory stick, but this is too small to store more than ten tracks of audio or more than three or four minutes of digital video. If you're serious about downloading to your PSP, you'll have to invest in a 512 Mb or 1 Gb Memory Stick Duo.

Copying media from your PC

Insert a memory stick into your PSP and then use a USB cable to connect the PSP to your PC. On the PSP's menu, browse to 'Settings' and then choose 'USB Connection'. Your PC should recognize it as a removable hard disk and you should now be able to drag and drop files.

Add photos

Select any number of JPEG files from your computer's 'My Pictures' folder and drag them into the 'Photo' folder on your PSP.

Add music

Adding music to the PSP is as easy as copying photos. Drag MP3 files from the 'My Music' folder into the 'Music' directory on the PSP. If you have songs and artists arranged in folders, you can copy those across too – the PSP will recognize them.

Add video

The PSP is more fussy about video files than it is with music or image files. It will only play MPEG 4 video (these have a .MP4 extension). They need to be copied into a folder called 100MNV01 inside the MP_ROOT folder on the Memory Stick.

On many video websites, you can download clips ready prepared in the PSP format, making transfer to your console effortless. There are also several tools available online to convert existing video to work on the PSP. Just search online for 'PSP video convert'.

Buying songs online

At the moment there's only one online music service that allows you to download music directly to your PSP – Sony's own Connect service. Although not as good as other outlets such as iTunes, Rhapsody or Napster, Sony Connect has a good selection of current and past artists. Tracks are competitively priced and once downloaded can be burnt onto CD, or copied to any Sony device, including their minidisc players and digital music players such as the NW–HD Walkman range (see page 64).

Unfortunately, since purchased tracks are in Sony's own ATRAC 3Plus format, it means that they're not compatible with iTunes, Windows Media Player or any other player on your computer.

want to know more?

• The PSP stores your saved games on the memory stick. If you're stuck in a game, you can download somebody else's saved game from a website such as psp-vault.com and copy it over.

• Songs that you have bought and downloaded from online outlets such as iTunes, Napster or Rhapsody will be copy-protected and may not work on your mobile phone, PDA or Xbox 360.

weblinks

• For all the PSP downloads you could need go to: www.pspworld.com or www.psp-vault.com/

• For everything Xbox go to: www.xbox.com

• Sync any mobile phone or PDA with iTunes www.nesfield.co.uk/ synctunes/ (Mac) http://ita.sourceforge.net/ (pc)

Glossary

AAC Apple's compressed digital music format. Better quality than MP3 files, AAC files can however only be played on iPods and in the iTunes player.

AIFF Apple's uncompressed audio format. Very high quality but enormous file sizes compared to MP3 files.

AVI Digital video format developed by Microsoft.

autoplaylist A playlist your computer generates of your digital music collection based on a set of criteria you decide. For instance, all tracks over three minutes by Madonna released between 1990–95. Also known as 'smartlists'.

BMP Microsoft's digital image format.

broadband A hi-speed Internet connection, often ten times faster than dial-up.

burning Internet slang for making your own CD using your computer.

CD-R Recordable CD that can be written to just once.

CD-RW Recordable CD that can be written and rewritten to many times. However, these do not play on all stereos or players.

clickwheel The circular controller used on iPods. Menus are navigated by stroking the clickwheel clockwise or anti-clockwise.

compression A technique for reducing the size of files. Compression is either 'lossless' where no data is discarded (used for programs and data), or 'lossy' where surplus data is discarded to make the file smaller (used for photos and videos).

dial-up A slow way of connecting to the Internet using a modem attached to a phone line. This system is too slow for downloading large files such as movies.

digitizing Converting anything (audio, video, images) into a digital file on your computer.

digital player Programs that allow you to sort and play the digital music on your computer, for example, Apple's iTunes and Microsoft's Windows Media Player.

DivX A very popular, very high quality digital video format online.

DRM Short for 'Digital Rights Management' which basically means 'copy protection'. Downloaded music files that contain DRM can only be played and copied in certain, restricted ways.

FTP File Transfer Protocol is a way of reliably downloading files from the Internet. You can have FTP sites, FTP programs and FTP downloads.

GIF A low quality image format used universally across the Internet.

gigabytes Used to denote the size of very large files on a computer such as downloaded movies. Hard disks are measured in gigabytes.

ID3 tags The extra data found in digital music files that contains essential information such as album name, release date, song length etc.

kilobytes Used to denote the size of very small files on a computer such as documents or photos. Around 1,000 kilobytes make a megabyte.

JPEG The most common digital photo format. Most digital cameras store their photos as JPEG files.

library This where all your digital music files are stored on your computer.

malware Any downloadable software that has the potential to harm your computer, for example, viruses, spam, spyware etc.

megabytes Used to denote the size of medium-sized files such as digital audio tracks. The average downloaded song is around 3–4 megabytes. Approximately 1,000 megabytes make a gigabyte.

MPEG The most common digital video format. It comes in several flavours (MPEG 1, 2, 4 etc.) which vary in quality.

MP3 The most common and popular compressed digital music format. MP3 files can be listened to on all computers and portable players.

playlist A list of audio tracks, grouped by album, genre etc.

plugins Small pieces of software that you can add on to programs such as Windows Media Player to provide new features.

podcast A radio show you can subscribe to via the Internet and then download and listen to whenever you want.

portable player Any gadget, such as the Apple iPod, that allows you to listen to your digital music collection on the move.

PSP The Playstation Portable video games console that can be used to play music and video files.

P2P A style of downloading where parts of the file is distributed across multiple computers rather than a single computer. Also known as 'file sharing' as P2P allows downloaders to share their files with hundreds, even millions, of others.

PVR Personal Video Recorders allow you to record hours of TV to their hard disks.

quicktime Digital video format from Apple that can be downloaded or streamed.

rating How many stars for quality you have given to an audio or video file on your computer.

real A streaming video format very popular online (comes in either 'video' or 'audio').

ripping Internet slang for converting the audio from a CD into digital music files on your computer. Also known as 'digitizing' and 'grabbing'.

shuffle A player mode that chooses random tracks one after the other.

skins New (often funky) designs that replace the default look (or 'skin') of Windows Media Player.

spyware Malicious software sometimes hidden in downloaded programs that pushes unwanted adverts or secretly transmits your personal data to commercial (or criminal) companies.

streaming Receiving a transmission of music and video from the Internet which, unlike a download, you can't keep or copy.

synchronization A process whereby the contents of the music library on your computer is automatically mirrored on your portable player.

tags Extra keywords and information you can add to a file to make it easier to sort. For example, the release date, artist and running time tags on music files.

TIFF A high quality digital photo format. Some top-of-the-range digital cameras can take photos in TIFF format.

trojans Pieces of 'malware' that disguise themselves as helpful files or attachments.

USB Stands for Universal Serial Bus and is used for connecting extra gadgets and technology (portable players, mice, keyboards) to computers. Most modern computers have two or more USB ports.

viruses Small programs that infiltrate computers and networks by making copies of themselves and spreading via emails and downloaded files.

visualizer A player mode that generates fast, colourful abstract images in time with the music.

WAV Uncompressed and high-quality audio format. It can be downloaded from some online music stores but the files are huge.

WMA Microsoft's digital music format. Higher quality than MP3 files but not playable on iPods or in Apple's iTunes player.

WMV Microsoft's digital video format.

ZIP files The most common form of 'compressed' files which have had their contents squeezed to make them easier to transfer across the Internet.

Need to know more

Further reading

Download ilounge.com's free iPod Book
www.ilounge.com/index.php/news/comments/ilounge-releases-the-free-ipod-book-22-for-immediate-download/
The Rough Guide to iPods, iTunes and Music Online by Peter Buckley, Rough Guides
The iPod Book: Doing Cool Stuff with the iPod and the iTunes Music Store by Kieber Stephenson, Peachpit Press
Podcasting For Dummies by Tee Morris, Hungry Minds, Inc.

Recommended websites

General
For all things iPod and iTunes:
www.ilounge.com
For the latest news on gagets, mobile phones and downloading technology:
www.engadget.com
For an explanation of the DRM (copy protection) found on many commercial downloads:
www.playsforsure.com
www.apple.com/support/itunes/music-store/authorization/
A review of online music download stores:
www.extremetech.com/article2/0,1697,178 4353,00.asp
A list of all current online music download stores:
http://en.wikipedia.org/wiki/Online_music_store

Video downloads
www.youtube.com
www.ifilm.com
www.atomfilms.com
http://video.google.com
http://video.yahoo.com
www.grouper.com
www.revver.com

Podcasting
Guides to making your own Podcasts
http://podcasts.yahoo.com/publish
www.apple.com/ilife/tutorials/garage-band/gb3-1.html
www.bbc.co.uk/radio1/onemusic/howto/download/podcastp01.shtml

Royalty free music for your Podcasts
http://music.podshow.com
www.thepodcasthotel.com
www.podsafeaudio.com
http://music.podshow.com

Podcast Directories
www.ipodlounge.com/
http://podcasts.yahoo.com/
www.podnova.com/
http://ipodder.org/
http://podcasting.meetup.com
www.podcastdirectory.com
www.podcast.net
www.podcastingnews.com
www.podcastpickle.com
www.podscope.com
www.podcatch.com
www.podcastcentral.com
www.podcastalley.com
www.syndic8.com
http://newtimeradio.com

Index

Index

⚙ Collins need to know?

Look out for these recent titles in Collins' practical and accessible need to know? series.

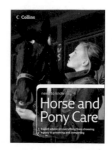

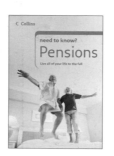

Other titles in the series:

**To order any of these titles, please telephone 0870 787 1732 quoting reference 263H.
For further information about all Collins books, visit our website:
www.collins.co.uk**